4 Weeks to an **Organized Life** with AD/HD

4 Weeks to an Organized Life
with AD/HD

Jeffrey Freed, M.A.T., and Joan Shapiro, M.D.

Taylor Trade Publishing

Lanham • New York • Boulder • Toronto • Plymouth, UK

Published by Taylor Trade Publishing
An imprint of The Rowman & Littlefield Publishing Group, Inc.
4501 Forbes Boulevard, Suite 200, Lanham, Maryland 20706

Estover Road, Plymouth PL6 7PY, United Kingdom

Distributed by National Book Network

Library of Congress Cataloging-in-Publication Data

Freed, Jeffrey.
   4 weeks to an organized life with AD/HD / Jeffrey Freed and Joan Shapiro. — 1st Taylor Trade Publishing ed.
      p. cm.
   ISBN-13: 978-1-58979-326-2 (pbk. : alk. paper)
   ISBN-10: 1-58979-326-9 (pbk. : alk. paper)
   1. Attention-deficit disorder in adults. 2. Attention-deficit hyperactivity disorder.
   I. Shapiro, Joan. II. Title. III. Title: Four weeks to an organized life with AD/HD.
   RC394.A85F686 2007
   616.85'89—dc22
                                    2007008891

Manufactured in the United States of America.

Contents

Contents

Acknowledgments

A **book may start** with a solitary inspiration, a vision, and an empty page. But its realization travels a sometimes circuitous path, and its production involves a team effort. Our team helped shape the final product, and kept this project going from the first inspiration to the final publication.

Our agent, Faith Hamlin, kept telling us to hang on, that everything would work out. It didn't always seem that way, but she was right. Knowing Faith, we never should have had any doubt!

Diane Stafford gave us new views on what has become second nature to us, and for that, as well as for her energy and professionalism, we are grateful.

P. J. Dempsey, our first editor, working in a situation full of difficulties about which we'll never know, really wanted to see this book in print, and worked to make that happen.

Rick Rinehart pulled up the rear, cheering us on through the final push, when we might have given up.

Jehanne Schweitzer and the staff at Rowman & Littlefield patiently got us up the technology learning curve.

Our patients and clients are the unsung heroes of this endeavor. Their suffering makes us want to work harder. Their growth and blossoming give us countless rewards. We know they need this book, because we've worked to help them, one by one, to play to their strengths.

Our colleagues, who get excited about our ideas, keep the energy going.

And, of course, we get continuous help from our families. We have no way of knowing how many things they didn't ask each of us to do because they would hear, "I'm working on the book." So we are, as always, deeply grateful to our families—Joan's husband George and daughter Laura and Jeffrey's wife Beth and son Jeremy.

4 Weeks to an **Organized Life** with AD/HD

Introduction

You picked up this book because you crave more order, more predictability, or more organization in your life. You probably have tried many times to get more organized, and in your quest for a workable plan, you've probably already devoured a number of books on this subject. But somehow, the "answer" remains elusive. You just can't seem to get a handle on what you're doing wrong—and worse, you can't zero in on a way to do better. The desire is in you, but you lack the right tools.

If there's one thing you know for sure, it's that your life doesn't work in the way it does for your friends, your spouse, your parents, or even your coworkers. Perhaps they remind you (as if you needed a reminder) that you are most consistent in making plans that you don't actualize, and promises that you break.

You have a history of being late for parties, dinners, and appointments, or missing them altogether. *You overpromise and underdeliver.* This bothers you, and it bothers the people who know you.

You disappoint not only other people, but also yourself. You forget things that are important to you, too. Your follow-through is terrible. You have inspiration that evaporates and energy that dissipates.

You get confused or overwhelmed by all that you see, so that you cannot pick out specific details, and can't orient yourself in space or time. You cannot find a starting point or identify your final goal. Without a beginning or an end, you don't have the structure to finish.

Been There, Done That

The authors of this book—both having attention deficit disorder (AD/HD) themselves—are no strangers to many of the scenarios described above. But that's only part of what led to this collaboration.

Jeffrey Freed, a much sought-after educator, had been working for years helping students with the special learning issues of giftedness and attention deficit/hyperactivity disorder (AD/HD). Joan Shapiro, MD, an experienced psychiatrist, was looking for ways to enhance her adult AD/HD practice. Working in the same field, they decided to meet. Curious because of what she had heard from people who had worked with Jeffrey, and because of his book, *Right-Brained Children in a Left-Brained World*, Joan drove into the Rocky Mountain foothills to meet with Jeffrey. Jeffrey figured Joan might also be a good resource, and it wouldn't hurt to see if she was a good psychiatrist.

It only took minutes to see eye to eye. Joan had been feeling that traditional psychiatry did not address some of the difficulties she saw in her patients. Many of the symptoms she observed did not seem to be the result of a mental illness, but rather of a mismatch between the way her patients made sense of the world and the way they were expected to make sense of it. Jeffrey did not like to see children with learning differences diagnosed with a psychiatric illness and treated with unnecessary medication. But he had begun to see the benefits that accurate psychiatric treatment provided in making it possible for many of his students to use his suggestions effectively.

As we talked about our work, we realized that, although coming from very different training and experiences, we saw the issues in much the same way. AD/HD, right-brain thinking, learning disabilities, hyperactivity, and hypersensitivity were related. We could see them on a continuum. We could see how they were misunderstood in both the educational and psychiatric communities, and we had a lot we wanted to understand and to share. In fact, we each had learned so many things that we hadn't seen written about anywhere that we both wanted to write another book.

Joan was seeing the results of lifetimes of both missed and misdiagnoses. She was perplexed and frustrated by the horrible stigma still attached to AD/HD, a stigma that left many people without the proper help.

Jeffrey had similar frustrations, seeing children with visual learning styles treated as "broken left-brainers," instead of as who they really are—right-brained, visual thinkers. He had developed more techniques and applications of his theories since his last book. But his literary agent had told him that his next book really should be written in collaboration with a psychiatrist.

Our combined experience was perfect. Could this be a team? As we sat across from each other at a library table, wondering if it could be this easy, the last piece fell into place: we shared the same literary agent! We each called Faith Hamlin. She said, "Do it!"

The left side of the brain, the logical, linear part, says this was a coincidental, but not remarkable, meeting of two people in the same field who live in the same part of the country. Our paths would eventually have crossed. There aren't a huge number of literary agents who specialize in psychology and self-help.

We should listen to the left side of the brain. It's what gets us to work on time, pays the bills, keeps our mouths shut when we'd rather say something nasty, and keeps things in order. It learns phonics and grammar. We like the left side of the brain.

But the right side is important, too. It's the part that stands out in the rain to see the biggest, brightest rainbow ever, even if we have to go to dinner with wet hair. It dreams the big dreams, without worrying about the details. It loves the smell of cinnamon, cries for joy, and makes us fall in love.

The left side said we had the qualifications to write this book. The right side said we had come together to do something special. Both sides are correct, because we need logic, predictability, and safety, and we also need magic and rainbows. In this book we will be looking at both sides of the brain, and at the need to use all the strengths we have in order to make the most of who we are.

Finding Your Groove

The purpose of this book, then, is to share with you some simple, yet powerful techniques to develop and harness the strengths of your visual, right brain to help you organize your life. Along with that, we will help you see how to use treatment for AD/HD to maximize your success.

In order for this to make sense to you, we will first explain the basics of understanding AD/HD and right-brain thinking. We'll show you why these brain differences lead to difficulties with focus and organization. We'll then present a program to build your skill in an easy, gradual manner, while strengthening your brain and body to make the most of these skills.

Before You Leave the Starting Blocks . . .

We recognize that you may want to jump right into the program without reading the explanatory material. It's not a complicated program, and it will work whether or not you understand why it works. But, since a right-brained thinker learns best by understanding the purpose and meaning, you might find it easier to stick to the program if you understand exactly why you are doing it.

Hoping and Dreaming

Remember how you used to feel in the first few weeks of each new school year? You were excited and motivated. "This year" you would keep up with your assignments. You had new notebooks, sharpened pencils, fresh book covers, and a clean desk. But when the newness and excitement wore off and the tedium set in, so did your old habits.

This often happens with your new organizational systems. Since they've been developed by and for left-brained thinkers, they have good linear strategies. And when their newness and your excitement about "finally getting your act together" wear off, so does their effectiveness.

Yet, here you are, again. We can thank the resilience of the human spirit, as well as the stubbornness of the AD/HD brain. You may call yourself "hopeless," but we have to assume that you have not yet given up all hope. You need something new, however, because you don't need more of what you have already tried. We won't disappoint you.

Knowing What It's Like to Have AD/HD

Not sure if you have AD/HD? Ask yourself how many of the following describe you and the way you live.

- *Your papers are in stacks.* You know (or think you know) what is in each stack, and nobody had better move them, or all is lost! You have heard people talk about "filing" their papers. But if you were to put your papers in a file, and then put that file in a drawer, they would be out of sight and, for all practical purposes, they would cease to exist.
- *You are creative.* Your ideas tumble from one to another. But all of this creativity easily ends up in chaos. You never know which it is going to be, chaos or creativity.
- *You see lots of possibilities.* This is great for creative problem-solving. However, this creates an insurmountable obstacle when it comes to getting organized, because it is so difficult to make decisions. It's easier to choose between three than between thirty-one flavors! In practical terms, you don't know what to keep and what to throw out, or what to do first and what to do later.
- *You want to get organized.* Unfortunately, when you try orga-

nizing methods that seem to work well for other people, you fail. So, that leads you to conclude the obvious, that you simply can't "do" organization. In fact, you're used to seeing the intangible concept of organization hanging out there in the air—a very appealing dream but one that's impossible for you to achieve.

These are typical difficulties for people with AD/HD. Whether you have one of them or all of them, they interfere with daily life in innumerable ways. If your life doesn't improve, people assume that you don't care or that you don't try. But the truth is that you do try, harder and harder, to fix your flaws. The problem is, if you are trying really hard at the wrong solution, nothing gets better.

There is no need to blame yourself if you are using the wrong solutions. You have been using the only ones that are available. And they are created by people who don't have trouble being organized. No wonder their ideas don't help you. They help people whose brains work entirely differently from yours.

AD/HD Is Not an Easy Ride

On a basic biological level, people without AD/HD have brains that naturally use efficient and direct processes to sustain attention, to focus, and to prioritize. People with AD/HD use entirely different brain pathways, which go about those tasks in indirect and inefficient ways. To put it bluntly, if you don't have AD/HD, you do things because they are important. If you have AD/HD, you do things because they are interesting.

Organizational strategies that assume a natural ability to decide what is important and make that a priority, and then carry it out, will not work for people who don't do either one of those things naturally. AD/HD people have difficulty deciding on which tasks have priority. And then they have difficulty finding the motivation to execute those tasks and sustaining the attention necessary to complete them.

But that is only part of the problem. There is another dramatic difference between people with and without AD/HD, an important one that is not usually highlighted in standard descriptions of AD/HD. That difference is the result of left-brain or right-brain dominance.

Right Brain, Left Brain

You use your entire brain, all the time. However, just as some of us are right- or left-handed, we each have a predominant mode of thinking, using mostly the right side of the brain or the left. Whichever mode we use affects how we *process, store, and retrieve information.*

- *Right-brained thinkers* are rapid-fire, nonsequential, visual thinkers. If you are a right-brained thinker, you see things from many angles, often at the same time. You are a holistic, big-picture thinker, who needs to know why you are learning something before you can absorb it. You are a dreamer, and you tend to be distracted easily by your own endlessly changing internal world, as well as by the external world.

■ *Left-brained thinkers* are more sequential and linear in their thinking, learning in a step-by-step process. If you are left-brained, you think more in words than in pictures. You are logical and analytical. You keep track of time, and you tend to plan and prioritize. You are likely to finish one idea or task before starting on another.

Most people with AD/HD are right-brained thinkers, and most people without AD/HD are left-brained thinkers. This creates profound differences in how each group operates in the world and organizes information. Organization comes naturally to you if you are a left-brained, linear thinker. But it is very difficult if you are a right-brained, visual thinker.

Understanding Right-Brain Thinking

If you are right-brained, you don't take things one at a time in a clear, obvious sequence. Your tendency to think of many things at once, or to see the same thing from many different perspectives, contributes both to your creativity and to your difficulty staying organized. And it makes left-brained, linear organizational strategies frustrating failures for you.

You may also notice that your life is not only overwhelming, but full of contradictions. You are quick at some things, and hopelessly slow at others. You are competent, but disorganized. You are creative, but do not meet your potential because you don't finish your projects.

In working with children with this different learning style, Jeffrey has learned that standard teaching methods don't work. He has found that using their visual learning style, however, has created virtual miracles. We don't promise miracles, but we do know that approaches that don't work for visual learners when they are children fail them when they are adults, as well.

Right-brained thinkers face the same frustrations time and again:

- You lose your sticky notes.
- You write lists, but forget to look at them.
- You refer to a list only to find you can't read your own handwriting!
- You file something in a drawer, which for you is equivalent to burying it in a time capsule.

Why People Don't "Get" You

If you have heard, "What's wrong with you?" countless times throughout your life, it's not surprising if you tend to put your energy into thinking about what you do wrong instead of what you do right. You may not think that you do anything right! But, in fact, you *do*.

You do need to play to your strengths. You can't regroup and become a left-brained thinker, nor would you want to. But you definitely can use your own way of thinking as an asset rather than a drawback.

Yes, organization requires sequential processing. But you, the right-brained thinker, can find a different way to put things in sequence. You can use your visual skills to straighten up your life. You can use your visual skills to create a picture of a sequence, and this is a form of organization that will work for you.

Focusing on What's Right about You

If you are right-brained, then your visual mind holds its information in pictures. But these are not ordinary pictures. These are extremely vivid images. You may not realize it, because you have lived your whole life with this kind of thinking. But you can use this ability to your advantage. Depending on your particular gifts, you might be able to call to mind a whole page of a book that you were studying, as if it were a photograph. You might be able to see a nonexistent thing in your mind's eye as if it were as real as the book you now hold in your hands.

This is something that you can take for granted. Or it is something that you can understand, cultivate, and mine for its benefits. We think that the ability to create and hold vivid images in your mind is a gift that you can use to your benefit. And we are going to show you how.

Capitalizing on Visual Thinking

Before you can create anything, you must create a picture of it in your mind. The more vivid the image, the more useful it is. When you can make that image vivid and real, as real as the thing itself, then you have created the potential to bring your vision into creative reality.

This is actually the wisdom of the ages, the habit of highly successful people, the technique used to think and grow rich. It's all the same, and it is something that great teachers have been saying in different ways for thousands of years: to get whatever it is that you want to have, you must first create a powerful image of it.

As a visual, right-brained thinker, this is where you will find your advantage. As we have said, most people with AD/HD are visual thinkers. That means that you think naturally in images. It is these images that have tremendous power, a power that usually is not available to left-brained thinkers. You already possess a skill that others have to struggle to attain. You just didn't know it, you didn't think about it in this way, and you never thought of the advantage this gives you.

Having the raw talent, however, is not enough. In order to capitalize on this gift, you must use this ability to visualize *actively*. This means that you must conjure up an image with such accuracy and vividness that the picture contains much of the clarity and detail of the thing itself. Learning to do this is what will turn this talent into a skill that is a very practical and powerful tool.

Part I

The Problem

1

What Is AD/HD, Anyway?

Telling the AD/HD Story

You witness a car accident, and the memory of it goes to one part of the brain. You learn how to make a chocolate soufflé, and that memory goes to a different location. Men are given a problem to consider, and they use one area of the brain. Women given the same problem use multiple areas. A child has one entire half of his brain removed to cure continuous seizures, and he can still learn to read, write, and speak, even though the normal brain uses both its halves to learn these skills. These examples show us that the brain is not a homogeneous mass, but an organ with specific functional areas.

Through the study of anatomy, research using electrodes to stimulate parts of the brain, patients with tumors, trauma, or surgeries removing certain sections of the brain, recent brain scan and other radiological techniques, and through ingenious psychological experiments, a variety of different brain functions have been found to have specific locations in the brain. Though not so long ago the specifics of how the brain fulfills its functions were only roughly understood, advances in technology have led to an explosion of detailed information about the brain.

Some of the most revealing new techniques are *functional*. This means that they show where activity is taking place in the brain while the person performs different tasks, thinks about different things, or is presented with different stimuli. These studies show clear differences between AD/HD and non-AD/HD brain function.

Confused and Overwhelmed

We think of AD/HD as causing problems in thinking and behavior. If you have AD/HD, you can't remember what you were supposed to get at the supermarket, or where you put your keys or your checkbook. You get confused and overwhelmed when you have to do more than one thing at a time. You blurt things out that you later regret. You put things off even though you know very well that you may pay a heavy price for your procrastination.

It's very likely you have been called irresponsible, thoughtless, or lazy. You and the people around you may see these as primarily character flaws. And yet, AD/HD is really a neurological condition that results from specific types of brain functioning. This particular type of functioning is strong in some areas, but weak in those areas requiring certain kinds of sequencing, prioritizing, inhibiting, and filtering. Now we have knowledge about brain function that helps us understand why AD/HD presents the problems for you that it does.

Many people, however, are quite skeptical that AD/HD truly exists at all as a real entity. Scientific studies don't convince them.

They don't see the problems of AD/HD as anything special and think that some people just don't force themselves to deal with their issues. Even with scientific evidence, they find it difficult to believe that other people cannot overcome the obstacles that they, themselves, have managed to master. Often, the most skeptical people are those who have AD/HD themselves and have managed to cope. They have had to drive themselves very hard to achieve what they have, and they can be quite unsympathetic toward others who haven't been able to muster the same strength and stamina. You may be one of these people, and you may be working very hard to prove that you can do whatever you have to do, that nothing is "wrong" with you, and that saying you have AD/HD is just an excuse.

But AD/HD is real. In this chapter we give an overview of the neurology and the psychology of AD/HD. In this situation, knowledge truly is power. More understanding can help you problem-solve and troubleshoot your own organizational difficulties, because you may find that understanding why you behave and feel the way you do can help you create better strategies for yourself.

If you see parts of yourself in the stories we tell in this book, it's because these stories are composites of real people. They illustrate the kinds of problems you very likely have. We don't mean to say that you are not unique, as an individual. We do mean to say that there are certain patterns in people with AD/HD that are very, very common.

The Forest or the Trees

Jacqueline was forty-seven, and her husband, Jim, wondered if she would ever get her act together. Though she held a master's degree in engineering, she never stayed at a job long enough to get promoted. There was often a reason for her to leave that, from her perspective, never had anything to do with her. Maybe the boss was a poor manager, the environment was bad, or the company was not up to her standards. Sometimes she left because she knew that her performance was not what it should be, and leaving on her own would preserve her clean record. Because of her qualifications, her enthusiastic presentation and her personal energy, she got hired easily, time after time. But her salary remained at an entry level, and she felt frustrated and unappreciated.

Her teenage sons ran circles around her, and her household was always on the edge of being out of control. Jim suggested that it might be better if she didn't try to work for a while. He'd had a number of promotions, and they could manage to maintain their standard of living on his salary. But staying home was even more difficult for Jacqueline. It seemed that the more she was there, the more chaotic her home was. And the more chaotic her home, the more irritable Jacqueline was.

From Jacqueline's perspective, she didn't have any particular problems. There was simply a lot to do in running her household. In fact, she prided herself on being able to multitask, though this was often a natural outgrowth of her distractibility. She prided herself on being "high energy," though those around her wished that she would occasionally just sit still.

Dedicated, but Discouraged

Jim loved Jacqueline, but he didn't enjoy living with her. It wasn't just the chaos. It was that Jacqueline was always on the edge of losing it and seemed to react more and more to minor frustrations. Often these reactions were aimed at Jim, whether or not he had anything to do with them.

Since both Jacqueline and Jim felt frustrated with their life together, they agreed that they needed some counseling. After a few sessions, their marital counselor observed a long history of frustration, irritability, and difficulty with follow-through on Jacqueline's part. She suggested that Jacqueline's problems could be related to AD/HD. This really hit a sore spot in Jacqueline, because she was tired of always being identified as the problem. After all, she worked her tail off all the time! And Jim might be calm and orderly, but he was demanding and particular, and not always a treat to live with, either. But she trusted her therapist and she loved her husband and children. She'd go see Dr. Joan Shapiro for an evaluation, get a clean bill of health, and then they could move on.

Papers sticking out of her purse, half her collar folded under, Jacqueline dropped into the chair in Joan's office fifteen minutes late for her first appointment, and caught her breath. Gathering herself, she got down to business and launched right into her story. She knew that, at times, she could be difficult to get along with. That was because she always expected the best of herself, and she had the same standards for other people. But she knew she didn't have AD/HD. She'd always been well behaved as a child. And she'd gotten good grades. In fact, she'd often been teacher's pet.

But the symptom checklists she'd completed for the evaluation revealed another side of her. She was always restless. She started lots of projects that she never finished. And there were some important tasks and projects she couldn't seem to start, even if they were important. She interrupted others when they were speaking. She spent a lot of time looking for things that she had lost. When she left the house, she found herself making several trips to the car to retrieve items that she just realized she had forgotten. And she was sensitive and irritable. Despite her many accomplishments, these problems had been present for as long as she could remember.

She agreed that these descriptions of her were accurate. True, she was driven and on the go all the time. She had a lot of different things that interested her. Nobody could remember everything all the time. Yes, she interrupted people. But she only did that when she had something really important to say. The behaviors highlighted on her checklist and confirmed in the interview were true. But they were just part of her personality. She had learned to live with them. Everybody had strengths and weaknesses that they had to manage.

Jacqueline was not happy to hear from Joan that, in her medical opinion, Jacqueline did in fact have AD/HD. The diagnosis felt like a criticism of her, and a sign that she was a failure, even though she had always tried her hardest at everything she did. And it didn't make sense to her. People with AD/HD were troublemakers and cutups, not hard-working, self-supporting women with master's degrees!

Many people are truly relieved to hear that they have AD/HD. It explains so many things about themselves. It is an "ah-ha!" experience for many. For others, as for Jacqueline, it is a confirmation of suspicions they had had of themselves that there was something "different" about them. Being told that she had AD/HD made her feel as if she were broken. And, yet, that didn't make sense either, because she had so much confidence in herself. Certainly there were some things she could do better than others, and her motivation depended on what it was she was doing. Nevertheless, she knew that if she tried hard enough, she could do just about anything.

Jacqueline's story reveals much of the confusion and misapprehension about AD/HD. People often think that if you can focus on one thing, you ought to be able to train that same focus on any other thing. But AD/HD is an interest-based attention problem. It varies depending on the context or situation for each individual. So, a person with AD/HD functions differently at different times and in different settings. This is a basic aspect of AD/HD. In other words, (and, of course, you can see this in yourself, if you have AD/HD) the symptoms show up in different intensities at different times.

Most people, however, assume that if at some times they have no symptoms, they could not have the diagnosis. This common misunderstanding turns a crucial factor of AD/HD on its head. The fact that symptoms are present at some times and not at others practically *defines* AD/HD!

Even knowing this, you might look at yourself and respond as Jacqueline did. You see your successes in some areas and assume that you ought to be able to generalize those successes to any area. You explain your inability to do so with logical and commonsense reasoning. You might have been tired, or you might have been overloaded with other things. Perhaps the activity wasn't interesting. Or, using explanations you have probably heard time and time again, you were just lazy and unmotivated.

Different Strokes for Different Folks

Because different people react differently to the same situation, AD/HD looks different in different people. This variability is another characteristic that often leads people to believe that it isn't a real condition. Without a black-and-white snapshot of what AD/HD looks like all the time in everybody, it's easy to say, "It's him and not me."

Of course, none of the behavioral descriptions of AD/HD are limited to any particular type of person or to any diagnosis. Taken by themselves, they are part of human nature. Some are negative, moral judgments, like "lazy" or "unmotivated." Some are the ordinary ups and downs of life, like being too tired or too busy with other things. Although the diagnostic criteria and patterns of behavior seen in AD/HD are specific, the behaviors themselves are not unique in themselves. This makes it easy to conclude that the problems someone like Jacqueline are experiencing are normal, not AD/HD.

Picking Up on a Pattern

But AD/HD is defined by a *pattern* of symptoms. You don't have AD/HD if you once had a problem with focus, concentration, or follow-through, or if every now and then you get overloaded or unmotivated. If you put things off every once in a while, then you don't have AD/HD. And if you have symptoms of lack of motivation or procrastination only when you are clinically depressed, you don't have AD/HD. But if you have AD/HD, you will find a pattern of symptoms and problems in your life, "for as long as you can remember."

Fitting the AD/HD Profile

How do you know if you really have AD/HD, as Jacqueline did? There is no substitute for a careful evaluation by an experienced clinician. However, if you answer six or more of these questions as "Yes," and you can see these patterns as *present for your whole life,* then it is likely that you do have AD/HD. And if you do, in fact, have diagnosable AD/HD, it means that you need to gain a clear understanding of how your brain works so that you can be as organized and successful in life as those around you who don't have AD/HD.

The AD/HD checklist:

1. Do you procrastinate, regularly putting off tasks that, for you, require a lot of mental energy?
2. Do you have difficulty completing tasks or projects?
3. Do you often forget or find yourself late for appointments?
4. Do you feel restless or full of nervous energy and compelled to do things?
5. Do you have trouble organizing yourself to do a complex task?
6. Do you fidget or squirm, needing to move some part of your body if you have to sit or keep still?

Consider, as well:

1. Do you find yourself lost in your own thoughts, even when someone is talking directly to you?

2. Do you have difficulty throwing things away, even if they have little value or specific usefulness to you?

3. Do you react quickly to conflicts?

4. Do you sometimes blurt things out and then wish that you hadn't spoken?

5. Do you take things to heart, finding yourself easily hurt and sensitive?

6. Do you find that most of these problems disappear when you have something fun or interesting to do?

A Map of the Brain

An explosion of brain research began in 1962 when the first "split brain" patient was studied. In a bold attempt to stop uncontrolled epileptic seizures, doctors had cut this patient's corpus callosum, the band of nerve fibers that joins the brain's left and right hemispheres. The surgery succeeded in controlling the patient's seizures. But how would he function, now that his brain halves, or hemispheres, had lost their usual connections with each other? It was known from animal research that information presented to the right side of the body through the brain was inaccessible to the left. Would the same be true in humans?

Dramatically, the facts were made clear in research conducted by Nobel Prize winner Roger W. Sperry, Michael Gazzaniga, and their colleagues. When surgically separated, the left and right brains did in fact operate as two separate entities, with different capabilities. The right brain could identify objects, but could not name them. Knowledge and recognition were present, but words were absent. The left brain could name objects but might not understand what they were.

In one experiment, the subject pushed a button signaling that an object had been shown to the right side of his brain. But, when questioned about it, he denied that there was anything there! Without the left side's participation, he had no way to label it or, apparently, to consciously "know" it. Were the right and left hemispheres two brains acting as one? Was one brain acting as two? The more we knew, the more we needed to know.

And the more we knew, the more we needed to change our earlier knowledge. For example, until very recently we thought that we were each born with all of the brain cells that we would ever have. Brain cells, unlike other organs like intestines and muscles, were thought not to regenerate themselves if they were damaged or destroyed. Now we know that some brain cells can regenerate, and new connections can be made between other cells.

We know that a kind of "pruning" of possible brain pathways takes place as learning occurs, so that brain development includes the limiting of infinite possibilities. And yet we know that the brain also is "plastic," meaning that it can change. One of the ways in which we see the relevance of this is that when one part of the brain is damaged, another part of the brain usually takes over all or part of that function. That is what happened in the young child who learned most of what he needed to learn with only half a brain.

Brain Imaging Breakthroughs

Advances in brain imaging (techniques that go way beyond ordinary X-rays) have yielded more fascinating information. PET (positron emission tomography) scans, SPECT (single photon emission computed tomography) scans, and fMRI (functional magnetic resonance imaging) scans are tools for "functional imaging studies." This means that they allow us to look at which parts of the brain are functioning or active during different activities. They can do this by creating images of blood flow (more flow meaning greater activity) and sugar metabolism (again, more sugar used meaning more activity) in the brain.

By using these techniques, researches have been able to see where in the brain activity is taking place when a person performs certain tasks, has certain kinds of thoughts or memories, or experiences certain sensations. Therefore, these kinds of scans can locate brain activity relative to brain structure. So, for example, we can see what parts of the brain are active when we are angry, when we try to concentrate, when we ad/hd a second task to a first one, or when we retrieve a memory. Recent research has even shown what part of the brain is active when we fall in love!

What Mapping Means for AD/HD

Because of these imaging studies, we know a lot about the AD/HD brain. We know, for example, that different parts of the AD/HD and the non-AD/HD brain are active when given a task that requires focus and prioritization. The prefrontal cortex, the end-point of the pathway of executive (as in to execute, to perform) functioning, is active in the non-AD/HD brain. Other parts of the brain, notably those in the parietal cortex, are more active in people with AD/HD.

We can also see that a person with AD/HD is likely to use the visual part of the brain, while a person without AD/HD does not. This visual way of thinking tends to involve more information and tends to be more creative. However, it is not the most efficient strategy for linear, sequencing tasks. The non-AD/HD brain is active in parts that are more efficient and that are specialized in sequencing and verbalization. This makes non-AD/HD people more effective at the ordinary tasks of planning and prioritizing.

These functional imaging studies also have revealed a paradoxical truth about the AD/HD brain. Most people with AD/HD are aware that they have to work harder than other people to accomplish the same task. You may recognize this, and can see that you sometimes wear yourself out with effort, and yet you might be frustrated at not accomplishing your goals. This makes sense, however, as imaging studies show us that the AD/HD brain gets less effective, rather than more so, the harder it tries to concentrate.

Chemically Speaking

For the brain to work, nerve cells need to communicate with each other. These nerve cells send information to each other through discrete bursts or packets of chemicals. These "chemical messengers," as they have come to be called, leave one cell and attach to another, triggering a chemical reaction in that second cell.

This chemical reaction causes a change within that cell which stimulates that cell to send its chemical messenger on to the next, and so on and so on.

These chemicals of the brain are known as "neurotransmitters." Specific neurotransmitters affect sensation, emotions, thoughts, and behavior. Differences in these basic mental functions are controlled by the levels of specific neurotransmitters. In ad/hdition, different neurotransmitters are active in different parts of the brain. Some of these neurotransmitters are central to brain activity and the resulting difficulties of AD/HD.

Not Enough Norepinephrine

One of these neurotransmitters is known as norepinephrine. In ad/hdition to stimulating alertness and attention, it acts as a regulator of memory and learning. In its regulatory role, its presence gives us functioning brakes. So, having enough norepinephrine allows us to think before we speak or act. It slows us down enough to consider what we really want to do, rather than to act impulsively.

By regulating, norepinephrine allows us to hold thoughts in mind in order to consider them in relation to other thoughts, and therefore to weigh and consider options, and to have continuity of thought. This continuity also leads to continuity of feeling and behavior, giving us a coherent sense of who we are and where we are going. Without enough norepinephrine, we have reactivity, irritability, impulsivity, restlessness or hyperactivity, as well as hypersensitivity. Sound familiar? People with AD/HD do not produce enough norepinephrine.

This deficit results in a kind of sensitive moodiness, or a reactivity to the immediate environment, so that you lose a sense of continuity. Instead, you are subject to the many ups and downs of ordinary life, and often feel only as good or bad as your last success or failure. It also leads to an internal sense of restlessness, a discomfort with just "being." It leaves you very sensitive to the physical and emotional environment. If this level of irritation becomes overwhelming, you might even explode. Or, to minimize those extreme reactions, you might find that you avoid many situations that others find quite tolerable, or even label yourself "antisocial" or say that you have "social phobia."

Without enough ability to control these brain processes, the AD/HD person often lacks the ability to control thought processes. Ideas come and go, jumping from one thing to another. You might describe your internal world as if you are watching a number of television screens at the same time, or as if you are watching a television on which the channels keep changing. You might be unable to shut off thoughts about what you need to do, or what you forgot to do, and find yourself plagued by constant worries. You might find that you are tired at the end of the day but can't sleep, because although your body is tired, your mind just won't quit.

Depending on Dopamine

The other neurotransmitter that is important in AD/HD is dopamine. Dopamine is required for an important part of "executive functioning," the ability to think about, plan, and execute an activity.

The executive function brain pathway has these steps:

- Initial thought of the task
- Plans for accomplishing that task
- Following through on the task

Starting down this pathway, you must have motivation for or interest in that task. When working well, these brain functions enable a person to complete tasks from beginning to end without losing interest or becoming distracted and led off track.

But people with AD/HD don't always have the necessary dopamine needed for these tasks, and without adequate dopamine, it's very hard to get started on something, even if you know you need to do it. Without adequate dopamine, you don't feel motivated to do much of anything, and you feel a listless kind of boredom, often a very uncomfortable feeling. Or you cannot finish something that you have started, but instead lose interest and move on to something else that seems more exciting or that grabs your attention.

However, *if* the activity is interesting or fun for you, or *if* you feel true urgency because of an impending deadline (such as a term paper due the very next day), *then* something very different happens. Adrenaline, the fight-or-flight hormone, gets produced by the state of excitement. With your body or mind stimulated to this degree, you know that something is important, and this stimulates the production of dopamine. And then, guess what? All of a sudden, you can focus and produce like crazy. At those times, you don't seem to have any symptoms of AD/HD at all!

Let us say this again, because it explains a lot: excitement or high interest stimulates the brain to create enough dopamine. The dopamine fires up the motivational pathway of executive function. You get started, you stay focused, and you finish. Low interest or excitement leaves you feeling unfocused, confused about what to do, and often kind of "blah."

Because the lack of dopamine results in a very uncomfortable, listless kind of boredom that verges on the feeling of depression, people with AD/HD end up doing things to get the adrenaline going in order to get the dopamine going. Sometimes this is as simple as waiting until the last minute to do things, because the urgency gives you the neurotransmitters you need to get things done.

Things that maintain your highly stimulated state might be:

- You keep very, very busy.
- You start lots of new projects.

Sometimes, things get a little more dicey:

- You might participate in exciting or risky sports such as snowboarding, motorcycle racing, surfing, bungee jumping, or rock climbing.
- If that's not enough, you might gamble, either literally, at casinos, or more figuratively, by living "on the edge."
- You might have a series of dramatic relationships in which you mistakenly equate excitement with love.

People with AD/HD without hyperactivity (known as the "inattentive type") often have a very difficult time. If you have this type of AD/HD, you don't have the natural energy to propel yourself into things, get focused, or get started. You might describe yourself as depressed or just unmotivated. If someone else drags you along to do something that you generally enjoy, you'll end up having fun. But you won't take many steps to plan things for yourself.

We hope you now can see that AD/HD has quite a variety of presentations. Everybody is different, and, in many areas, what interests one person doesn't interest another. People are passionate about different things, and those are the things that will get their energy and attention.

And this is why you might often hear (or say to yourself), "You could do it if you really wanted to." This is true, but clearly not for the reason implied by these accusatory comments. Rather, it is true because your unique and personal interest will help you do a number of things that matter to you because of production of enough dopamine.

A Few More Chemicals

Other neurotransmitters, less central to what are known as the "core symptoms" of AD/HD, contribute to variations in symptoms in individuals with AD/HD. Serotonin, GABA (gamma-aminobutyric acid), and glutamine are some that are important. Serotonin, for example, is important for a stable mood, and for a certain kind of flexibility and tolerance. When lacking, you can see irritability, or difficulty switching from one thought or from one activity to another. GABA and glutamine are largely inhibitory neurotransmitters, necessary for mood stability and processing of external and internal stimuli.

Meds Can Help Most AD/HDers

In this context, we can see how medications help with the symptoms of AD/HD (see appendix for specifics). They help correct the imbalances in the neurotransmitters. For example, stimulants, a mainstay of the medical treatment of AD/HD, work by basically stimulating the production and release of dopamine and norepinephrine. People have found it curious that a stimulant would calm down a child with AD/HD and have thought of this as a paradoxical response to the medication. But it is not paradoxical at all. The medication causes the release of *inhibitory* neurotransmitters as well as those required for *executive functioning*.

Nonstimulant treatments work to decrease the removal of the neurotransmitters. Over several days or weeks, they shift the balance of creation and breakdown of the neurotransmitters, thus allowing a consistently higher level to be present. All of these medications, then, allow for better self-control, better working memory, and better ability to focus, sequence, and prioritize.

Medications do not "cure" AD/HD, because they do not cause a permanent change in the levels of neurotransmitters. But they can lead to long-term improvement because by improving a person's neurochemistry, they allow more learning and growth to take place. When this happens, people are often able to learn to live in more effective ways, to make changes that are appropriate for them, and to learn strategies such as the program we have created.

AD/HD and the Human Genome

Many people find it disconcerting to think that our personalities are determined by our genetic structure. We want to think that we determine our own paths in life, rather than to think that our biology defines us. But both are true. We are the physical product of our genes, which control not only physical traits and physical illnesses but also our personality traits and mental illnesses. Genes create the brain structure that we have. This basic structure is then affected by our environment, our choices, and our experiences.

Experts estimate that about 50 percent of what we would call "personality" is a direct result of our genetic makeup. Many psychological traits and mental illnesses are hereditary in nature. We take this for granted, of course, when we note a family resemblance, or when we expect a professional basketball player's children to be tall. We seem a bit less comfortable with the idea that psychological traits can also be inherited.

Some traits are more likely to be inherited than others. Height and intellectual ability are known to be fairly highly heritable, and anxiety disorders and schizophrenia are also seen to have strong genetic components. AD/HD, we find, is one of the more highly heritable of human characteristics. Research shows that it is almost as highly heritable as height.

When someone says, "My son couldn't have AD/HD, because I was just like him, and I don't have it," that often turns out to be a statement more revealing than the speaker intended. Most adults with AD/HD don't know they have it (it is estimated that at the beginning of 2007, only about 20 percent of adults who have AD/HD have been diagnosed). So the father's comment is entirely under-standable. However, awareness of AD/HD in adults is increasing. What often happens now is that when the son is diagnosed with AD/HD, the parent says, "If he has it and he's just like me, then maybe I have it." And that's right, because the likelihood of an AD/HD child having at least one AD/HD parent is pretty high.

Scientists have been mapping genes for years, looking for the lo-cations of disease-producing genes, often in the hopes of using that information to tailor treatments. Some studies have been com-pleted, and others are underway, to examine the genetics of AD/HD. The studies that have been done have revealed some consistent findings, showing that individuals with AD/HD have differences in dopamine-regulating genes compared to non-AD/HD individuals.

Always Needing Something New

People with this genetic structure seek higher levels of excite-ment than those without that particular genetic structure. They re-quire more stimulation to get dopamine production going. Because of that, they are attracted to ever more stimulating environments. And they seek out new and different stimuli. This gene, then, has been called the "novelty-seeking gene." It explains the large num-bers of motorcycle racers, downhill skiers, snowboarders, rock climbers, gamblers, and substance abusers in the AD/HD popula-tion.

Quite a bit has been written in recent years about the adaptive value of the trait of novelty-seeking. Exploration and invention are two natural outgrowths of this trait. People with these traits, including many famous figures in our history like Edison and da Vinci, would probably be diagnosed with AD/HD if they were alive today. So there are clearly positives that come from the desire to find new frontiers.

On the other side, the craving for more stimulation is related to a fragmented and scattered style. The current reality just isn't enough. The relentless urge to find something more or different makes it very difficult to manage the ordinary, mundane, and downright boring and tedious requirements of ordinary life. This biological drive to seek out new horizons often leaves the current environment in disarray, with unfinished projects, unpaid bills, and unmet promises.

And All of This Means . . .

- AD/HD is a real, biological condition.
- AD/HD's location in the brain can be seen in imaging studies.
- The neurochemistry of AD/HD can be described.
- The symptoms of AD/HD can be defined.
- AD/HD is highly heritable.
- AD/HD looks different in different people.

No one problem caused by AD/HD is unique to it. Rather, it is the pattern of difficulties, the intensity and frequency of them, the consequences of them, the impairments caused by them, and the lack of some other cause for them that lead to a clinical diagnosis of AD/HD. Any one of the individual difficulties can be found from time to time in anybody.

Any of the symptoms of AD/HD can be described in moral and judgmental terms. Lazy, irresponsible, and unreliable are the kinds of judgments made of people with AD/HD. These are seen as personality problems and they are, therefore, things that these people could fix, if they really wanted to. The fact that they don't fix these things reinforces the perception that these people are deficient.

We can summarize by saying that AD/HD is a context-dependent, neurologically based, data management problem that has psychological manifestations. And these are:

1. Problems with attention
2. Problems with focus
3. Difficulty with follow-through and completion
4. Distractibility
5. Hyperactivity
6. Irritability
7. Impulsivity
8. Emotional reactivity
9. Risk-taking behavior
10. Problems with motivation

"Go!"—The Default Position

You may have noticed in yourself, or in others you know with AD/HD, a habit of jumping into things. If something sounds like a good idea, you say "yes" to it before you have thought it through. If there is a crisis, you act, sometimes so quickly that you miss a simple solution in favor of the one that came to mind most quickly.

There is always a lot to do, so in order to stay productive, you keep busy. Knowing how behind you are, you might not ever feel okay about resting or "goofing off," because you have never really earned it. You do rest, eventually, but it's more like crashing after you have worn yourself out.

Perhaps because you hate the boredom of sitting still, you make sure you are always doing something. Because you crave stimulation, sitting and watching a television show or a recorded movie is something you cannot do without simultaneously doing something else. Perhaps you keep moving because you know that if you stop, it will be hard to get started again.

And, when it comes to general organization and making sense out of your life, you may feel overwhelmed and disorganized. However, knowing how much you have to do, you keep moving. That way, you are always doing something.

Each of these scenarios is a version of the tendency of many people with AD/HD to act without thinking things through. This tendency is related to the impulsivity, the distractibility, and the difficulty with sequencing associated with AD/HD. It also relates to the tendency that you may also notice in yourself to have difficulties in states of arousal versus rest. For example, you have difficulty going to sleep even if you're tired, because your mind won't quit even though your body is worn out. Or, you can't get started in the morning, even after a good night's sleep, because you just feel too groggy or lethargic. You're sleepy when you should be awake and awake when you should be sleepy.

Sometimes it seems as if there are no gradations for you. You're either at full steam ahead or stop. And much of the time, the dial is set to "go!" That's what we mean by the "default position." And this is part of the difficulty you have with organization and structure in your life: you keep busy, but you don't necessarily have a plan. It's as if your resting position is active, whether it's an active body or an active mind.

You leave the house for work without stopping to make sure you have everything you need. Then in what John Ratey, coauthor with Edward Hallowell of *Driven to Distraction*, calls "the pirouette sign," you turn right around and go back to get what you forgot. You get so busy doing something absorbing that you forget to do what you meant to do that was most important.

The Good with the Bad

It's time to flip things over for a moment and look at AD/HD from the other side. Since there are always two sides to every coin, it is very important never to forget that there are gifts that go along with the deficits of AD/HD. Impulsivity can also show up as spontaneity. High energy can show up as enthusiasm and optimism. Oversensitivity can manifest as true empathy. Thinking of too many things at once leads to inventiveness, humor, and an entrepreneurial spirit.

In ad/hdition, one of the important concepts that we want you to grasp as you work with new ways to understand yourself is that the body and brain are naturally self-balancing. So, if there is a weakness in some area, another area takes over. Though you have clear deficits in one kind of ability to organize, you can find strengths with which to overcome those deficits.

Visual thinking, the subject of the next chapter, is one of those gifts for most of you. So, as you understand some of the weaknesses causing your disorganization, remember that we will be showing you some strengths, as well.

A Recipe for Disorganization

Organization requires planning, getting started, staying with it, and finishing. Each of those crucial functions is disrupted by AD/HD. With deficiencies in each of these areas, disorganization is inevitable. Realistically, it is the norm.

Remedies for this disorganization have come from two directions. Either you can work to change the specific underlying symptoms, or you can change the context that determines the expression of those symptoms.

Treating the symptoms with medication, proper nutrition, sleep, rest, relaxation, and exercise all help improve focus and mental stamina. They increase emotional and frustration tolerance, and they help increase physical energy and sense of well-being.

The other approach is to change the conditions that produce the symptoms of AD/HD. Recognizing that some settings and situations are less confusing than others, some activities are more challenging than others, you can try to set up your life to include more beneficial settings and activities that give you a greater likelihood of success.

These are things that you have probably figured out, to some degree. If you get distracted by noise, then make it quiet. If visual distractions get you off track easily, then find ways to block off the visual distractions. If you get more flustered as the day goes on, then do your most difficult tasks in the morning.

If you can identify your areas of weakness, then you can get help with those areas. Coaching can help in staying on track. Standard strategies that are understood in AD/HD treatment communities include setting up structures, breaking tasks into small pieces, rewarding achievements, and learning to set priorities.

These strategies are numerous. One size does not fit all, but many are worth trying to see if they do fit. These ideas are covered in many, many books about managing AD/HD, and they are worth careful study. You never know when you'll discover just what works for you.

This is where our approach fits in, and yet our approach is very different from what you are used to. Most of the commonly used strategies are remedial. They look at deficiencies and then suggest ways to compensate for those weaknesses. It is, of course, important to remediate what you can. But what most approaches do is the same thing that remedial education programs for children do: they define you as "broken" and have you spend your energy in fixing your brokenness.

The remedial approach makes you put your energy into the areas in which you have the most difficulty and in which you repeatedly fail. This takes a lot of energy, can be painful, and is very difficult to sustain. Working the hardest at what you do the worst is demoralizing. Things that are supposed to be easy, and that are easy for other people, are very difficult for you. So, the experience of working in these areas is exhausting, discouraging, and, sadly, very familiar.

However, we are going to help you use your strengths to change the whole setting or context of organizational challenges. We are going to help you use your strengths to create an entirely different type of organization, one that does not constantly work against your grain.

Working in an area of strength changes everything. Achieving success changes even more.

Satisfying the AD/HD Brain

As we have said, AD/HD is an interest-based attention problem. If you are fascinated by or passionate about something, then you don't have any problem paying attention. In fact, you might even do what is called "hyperfocus." When you do this, you concentrate so hard on something that the rest of the world is virtually nonexistent. You may find that you tune out everything, including the people you live with and your own physical needs to eat and sleep.

But, when it comes to the tedious, the mundane, and the just plain difficult, nothing can get you to do it. The satisfaction of the completed task is just not, in itself, enough of a reward to get you to do it, because the pain of the effort is greater than the satisfaction of the end result.

Because of this selectivity of attention, people with AD/HD are often seen as selfish, immature, and only interested in fun. From the outside, you may seem to seek only rewards. It is ironic, then, that you can be the worst at rewarding yourself. You know that you are not doing what you are supposed to be doing, and you are your own worst critic. You live in a constant state of shame, blaming yourself for whatever goes wrong. Or you may go to the opposite extreme in order to avoid the pain that you feel, and end up blaming everyone else or the world around you for your difficulties. You may live as if you need to eat your vegetables before you can have dessert, and so you never feel that you have earned a reward. Or, you may go to the opposite extreme, eating dessert first!

You probably have a fantasy that someday you will "get it together." Then you can reward yourself. There are two problems with this reasoning if you have AD/HD. One is that, no matter how well you manage your AD/HD, it is never going to go away completely. You are going to forget things, lose things, and get your priorities backwards. Your fantasy that you are going to "get it together" is the fantasy that you will have a different brain. No chance of that! The second problem with this reasoning is that in this ever-changing, and more and more complicated world, it is not even *possible* for everything to get together.

As we move from understanding AD/HD and visual thinking to our unique program for you, we are going to ask you to reward yourself for each step that you take. We understand that this is difficult, and there are specific reasons why this is difficult for people with AD/HD to do. Understanding the nature of this difficulty along with the importance of creating rewards are important in making this program a success.

If you are a right-brained, AD/HD, visual thinker, you have the tendency to think all or nothing, black or white. You've either succeeded, and you've earned a reward, or you have failed, and you don't deserve one. But end results are not the only things that are important in life. The process is vitally important. The process is the small first step of a journey of a thousand miles.

There are many things in life that you cannot control, things from both your external and your internal world. Yet you do have some control over the effort you put out. And you need to reward yourself for that effort, no matter what the results. As you learn to focus on your strengths and harness your gifts, you will need to learn to reward yourself for your small steps and for your efforts.

If these reasons for rewarding yourself don't convince you, how about this: all work and no play will make your brain function worse. Stress impairs memory. Stress makes AD/HD symptoms worse. The more severe the stress, the more inefficient the brain, and the fewer organizational skills will be available to you. And, the truth is, fun is fuel for the brain.

Finally, you are going to go through a training program, and you need something to aim for that is more appealing, more immediate, and more satisfying to the AD/HD brain than the simple satisfaction of the completed task.

To make the rewards work for this program, they should be unique and special. They should be things that you wouldn't ordinarily do for yourself. That way, you can get a new and instant reward for doing something in this program that you have not done before. So, for example, let's say that you are on a very tight budget, but you love a good beer. You only buy the cheap stuff. For your reward, go to the liquor store and buy one or two bottles of special beer. Put it in the refrigerator. Put a mug in the freezer. And only open the beer when it is time for one of your rewards.

It is likely that what you do not give yourself is time. For a special reward, you may not need to spend any money. You may need to go downtown to some galleries. You may need to watch the kids feed the ducks in the park. You may need to go to the zoo by yourself, without taking a child along. Your reward might be an hour of *guilt-free* video gaming. It might be a pedicure, a cheesesteak, signing up for art lessons or salsa dance lessons. Whatever it is, it should be something that you don't usually let yourself do, but that you can now associate with putting in the effort to make this program work for you.

Changing the Emotional Context of AD/HD

If you are like a lot of people with AD/HD, you are used to expecting failure and criticism. Or you set your sights low, so that you won't be disappointed in yourself. The whole idea of AD/HD is, honestly, not a good thing.

Common words that are used to describe people with AD/HD (and that you might have heard describing you) include, but certainly are not limited to, lazy, selfish, unmotivated, sloppy, disorganized, spacey, forgetful, narcissistic, flighty, absentminded, stupid, irresponsible, and unreliable. People might say that giving a diagnosis as a cause for these failings is just an excuse. Again, there is the familiar criticism that you could change these things if you really wanted to.

But the inner experience of having AD/HD is anguish and frustration at not being able to do the things you want to do or to be the person you want to be. You often use the same negative terms to describe yourself as others use to describe you, and wonder what's wrong with you because you can't do what you know you should.

The diagnosis is not a blank check for irresponsibility and immaturity. It is, however, an explanation that can lead to treatments and effective strategies for change. In addition, blame and shame are not only useless, they are destructive. They make change less likely, not more likely. The pressure caused by judgments results in the same kind of problem in the AD/HD person as we see when you are asked to perform tasks that you are poor at. The harder you try, the worse you do.

Success and positive reinforcement, however, lead to better performance. They allow you the space to more critically evaluate yourself. They make the defenses against the feelings often less necessary. The energy that has gone into keeping those terrible feelings at bay is now available for positive change.

AD/HD brings its problems. The more actively they are dealt with, the better the likelihood of success and satisfaction. And we can keep in mind the gifts that accompany the difficulties of AD/HD. The hyperactivity brings with it positive and enthusiastic energy. The sensitivity brings empathy and concern for other people and the world. The distractibility brings the ability to think of unusual juxtapositions of things that produce the life-changing inventions as well as the great comic geniuses we all enjoy. The right-brain thinking that brings huge potential for visualization also brings the possibility for great focus and determination. And that will allow for much better organization.

2

Picture This The Visual Thinker

What Is a Visual Thinker?

There is no doubt that although the brain is a single organ, it has different parts or functional components that all work together to form a unified whole. By having the right and left hemispheres specialized to perform different functions, the brain gets more power in less space.

As we have said, the right brain is responsible for spatial orientation, for understanding relationships of all kinds, and for certain kinds of creativity. It can evaluate and imagine things from many different angles, and it sees connections, similarities, and parallels. It makes jokes and puns. It uses images. It recognizes objects by their properties and meanings, but it does not name them. It is aware of various sensory modalities, such as taste, touch, and sound, and it registers, usually out of the conscious awareness, signals from the body's internal organs.

Right-brained thinkers are gifted in spatial intelligence. There are many different forms of spatial intelligence. One form allows us to visualize and manipulate objects in space. With this ability, some of us can, for example, view a broken piece of equipment and examine it mentally from different angles and figure out what's wrong.

It is interesting how something that is an ability in one context is a disability in another. Ronald Davis has been at the forefront in bringing this reality to light. In *The Gift of Dyslexia*, he describes dyslexia as a right-brain condition. Seeing things from different angles can be helpful in seeing things from different perspectives. But it can make reading difficult, for example, because it is not easy to tell a "b" from a "d," as they are mirror images of each other.

Another form of spatial intelligence involves interpersonal intelligence. If you are a right-brained thinker, your ability to view things from different perspectives allows you to view social situations from different angles. Potentially, this can be useful because it enables you to view things from another's perspective and have empathy. Or it can enable you to view yourself from others' perspectives, and use this to understand relationships.

Sometimes this tendency to view social interactions from different angles can become overwhelming. There are so many different ways to look at a single situation that it is difficult to know which perspective is the most realistic. If your brain works this way, you might find that you can get so overloaded and anxious by all of this information when you are around other people that you complain of having "social anxiety disorder." Sometimes, just understanding how your brain works makes so much sense of your experience that you might find that you are no longer overwhelmed.

Visual thinkers are very sensitive and experience many things more acutely than others. Sounds, smells, textures, buzzing, and vibrations can be very disruptive. Emotions can also be very disruptive, because you may feel them so intensely. These emotions can be your emotions or the emotions of other people. You might feel that other peoples' feelings seem to get "inside" you, and you might, at times, isolate yourself, for your own protection.

Right-brained, visual thinkers are rapid-fire thinkers, whose ideas can take off in many directions. Sometimes this leads to great performance, as when quick responses are important. Sometimes it leads to impulsivity. Usually, a visual person's mind is quite active. In some circumstances, you might find this to be enjoyable. The ideas you have can connect with each other to lead to creativity, inventiveness, and humor. You might laugh out loud at something you've thought, without even realizing it. But you also may find that at other times the ideas diverge so much or move so quickly that the only result is cognitive and emotional chaos and disorganization.

These characteristics are aspects of intelligence. Described by Howard Gardner in *Frames of Mind*, different kinds of intelligence are found in different people. Some of them are more prominent in left-brain thinking and some in right-brain thinking. Since the mind is an organ that naturally aims for organization and order, these forms of intelligence are used to make sense of the world. In a person with left-brain prominence, thinking of things in steps and in categories are ways to make sense of the world. Sequencing and prioritization are natural, easy, satisfying, and relatively automatic ways of thinking.

But a person with right-brain dominance uses other aspects of intelligence to order and demystify the world. Though it does not help much with prioritizing, gathering lots of information from many different sources gives a broad orientation. Being able to scope out a situation by seeing it from different perspectives is a useful skill in daily life. It has also been adaptive human evolution. Not that long ago in our history, relatively speaking, we all lived off the land. Awareness of all that was around us helped orient us to what was required in that world, and this skill often would mean the difference between life and death.

These differences in styles of thinking and different types of intelligence are highlighted in an extremely illuminating way by Thom Hartmann, who has written about AD/HD from the perspective of its adaptive advantage. In *Attention Deficit Disorder: A Different Perception*, he describes the differences between the "hunter" and the "farmer." Very briefly, Hartmann convincingly proposes that the farmer finds it useful to be linear, repetitive, and regulated to be successful at planting, cultivating, and harvesting. The hunter finds it advantageous to be extra sensitive, reactive, and hyperfocused to be successful at stalking, hunting, and killing his prey. Very different in skill and style, each type has its use.

In our current culture, each style has its advantages and uses. However, most advantages still go to the left-brained thinker who can stay organized despite distractions, and can do what is expected when it is expected. The creative, sensitive, impulsive person doesn't rate highly in this world. And this sensitive, creative, intuitive, emotional, impulsive, and highly interest-motivated person does poorly at organizing a complex life.

Visual Thinker as Visual Learner

Many people think that a visual learner is someone who needs to see things in order to learn them. But that is not exactly what we mean. The term "visual learner" really refers to the way an individual stores information, not to how he or she takes in that information.

To visual learners, seeing something and then just remembering it can be the most straightforward path to learning something. If you are this type of learner, all that is required is that you truly "pay attention" when you are looking at something you are attempting to learn.

But, if you are a visual learner, you can also process well through auditory and kinesthetic means. What you have to do in these circumstances is to focus on the information, and consciously and intentionally turn the material into a mental image.

Auditory learners are different in that these left-brained people process information more like a tape recorder, and remember the information in a more verbal and linear fashion. Because they visualize relatively poorly, they must write things down and make lists. They must have these lists in convenient places and they refer to them regularly. This is fine for them as typically they have legible handwriting, they think in steps that make their lists useful, and they put their lists in places where they can locate them.

The visual learner's brain cannot easily remember sequential things or logically figure out where they put something. Their rapid-fire visual brain gets impatient when writing things down, their hands often get tired when writing, their lists get placed in illogical places and cannot be quickly located.

There is considerable overlap between the difficulties associated with AD/HD and with visual learners. In both situations, linear thinking is difficult, prioritization is a problem, and the mind is distracted by many different thoughts and stimuli.

Most people with AD/HD have a predominantly visual learning style. You can have AD/HD without being a visual learner. You can be a visual learner without having AD/HD. However, most commonly, there is overlap.

There is, of course, a continuum of both conditions. When it comes to right-brain thinking, some people are so right-brained that they joke that they "don't have any left brain at all!" And some are predominantly right-brained, but with workable left-brain skills that they can access, even if with some difficulty. There are degrees, then, of organizational difficulties that AD/HD people experience. The common pathways, involving basic neurological functioning, however, are similar.

Why Organization Is a Challenge

Maybe you are like Emily, wondering why nothing was helping her get her life in order. She would joke, sometimes, with her sympathetic friends: "There are drugs to help make you less compulsive. Why aren't there drugs to make you *more* compulsive?" (She didn't know that, in a way, there are. They are medications that treat AD/HD.)

Desperately, Emily wanted her life to be in order, but she never could seem to make it happen. She was productive, to be sure, in plenty of other areas, able to channel her energy and accomplish

quite a lot. Her teaching career had led to her promotion to princi-
pal of a high school. She played the violin in the community or-
chestra. She was married and the proud and happy mother of two
children. She and two of her friends were training for a half-
marathon. It was quite a list of accomplishments.

On the outside, she was admired and respected by all. On the
inside, though, she felt she was always playing catch-up. She had an
unremitting feeling that she had forgotten something, though she
couldn't remember what it was. She knew she could never quite
keep track of things, whether concrete things like keys and phone
numbers, or thoughts like lunch plans or ideas she wanted to bring
up at a meeting. It was as if she were the plate spinner on "The Ed
Sullivan Show."

Her house appeared tidy enough. It was important to her that
she be seen as a good housekeeper. But you could look in any
drawer or cabinet, and you would see chaos. She wished that,
someday, she could get organized. But she felt hopelessly organiza-
tionally impaired. And she saw it as a character flaw. She felt
ashamed of this deficit. She worried about the day when, surely,
people would discover the truth about her.

Or, maybe you are more like Emily's husband, Alex. Alex
would just stand by, watching her get bent out of shape over little
details that made very little difference to the big picture. Fairly
easygoing and low-key, he thought that the two of them were very
different. Emily worried about scheduling and details. Alex thought
she got herself worked up over things that weren't all that important. Emily liked to plan lots of things in advance. Alex liked to
take things as they came. He thought that he and Emily had con-

nected because opposites attract. He didn't realize how alike they really were.

Alex worked as a computer systems consultant. A history major in college, he had a master's degree in business. But as far as computers were concerned, he was largely self-taught. He had ended up in his current career because he had a natural feel for how networks needed to be set up. Presented with a company's needs, he could envision the system that would work best for them. Confronted with a system's glitches, he could easily see where the problems were likely to be and suggest remedies. He had tried running his own company for a while. But the details of running a business— personnel, billing, tax filings, and business development were not his cup of tea. He did better working for someone else, just doing what he enjoyed doing.

The ease with which Alex performed his work allowed him to ignore his shortcomings. He had been unable to run his own business because he just couldn't seem to get those details to be under his control. All of the requirements seemed to hit up against each other. He never could tell which task was most urgent, and he therefore found himself putting out fires, skipping routine tasks, and never feeling caught up. It was much more comfortable for him to let someone else handle those details and work for less money.

Because Alex also let Emily handle the details at home, he didn't realize that he would have been just as overwhelmed as she was in that role. His visual thinking was what made him so gifted at troubleshooting computer networks. He had a picture in his mind that he could study as if it were a manual. He could look at it from any angle. He could see it beginning with the first page or with the last page. All the possibilities were available to him and all he had to do was pick one that would work.

The problem was that he saw everything from all those angles. He could see all of the tasks required to organize a home, as well. Should he do the cleaning or take out the garbage or call to make an appointment with the pediatrician or pay the bills? The ideas went back and forth in his head the way they did when he was trying to run his business, and he couldn't figure out if he should work on the budget or on advertising.

Alex and Emily are two bright people, each with AD/HD and a right-brained, visual thinking style. They are both creative and have a variety of interests. When doing what they do well, they excel, and often get into a state of flow. But, when it comes to the tasks of daily living, they are pretty deficient. And we can see why.

Details overwhelm them. Their nonlinear, creative, high-speed brains lead them to a lot of interesting things in their lives. But the routine and the repetitive, they don't just find disagreeable. They find them impossible.

They have different styles of coping with this. Emily tries very hard to master those details, and Alex structures his life to avoid them. Emily tortures herself with her deficits. Alex has convinced himself that his don't matter. Emily's frustrations are more bothersome to her than to others. Alex's problems are invisible to him, but they are very annoying to Emily, who's filling in for him despite the fact that she's working in an area of her own deficiency.

Yet, each has gifts. Emily excels at teaching because her empathy and creativity enable her to evaluate, moment by moment, what will help her students. Alex excels at his computer work because his visual-spatial skills enable him to diagnose problems and create unique solutions.

Disability versus Difference

Our medical model is one of disease, not wellness. It is a system that asks, "what's wrong?" rather than "what's right?" To warrant a diagnosis of AD/HD, an individual is identified as having a minimum number of symptoms. Then they get a diagnostic code, a label. This pathological view of what many see as simply as normal human variation keeps many people with AD/HD from getting help that would enhance their lives and help them be more of who they really are.

A pathological view ignores the gifts that accompany AD/HD. There is no requirement to identify any of these gifts in making the diagnosis! These gifts are what we are going to use to help you get more organized. But they are, at the same time, part of the problem. To channel them productively, it helps to see how they can take you down a path of disorganization, so that you can guide these gifts in a useful direction. Right-brained, visual thinking is responsible for many of the struggles of AD/HD people to get or to stay organized.

All Angles, All the Time

We can see, then, that if this ability to see from different angles is not harnessed, it can yield confusion. All of that information from all those angles can leave you not knowing which end is up. If you keep changing the direction from which you are looking at something, there is no obvious starting point. Not having a starting point certainly makes it hard to get started! You might not know how to recognize the end any more than the beginning.

If you easily go back and forth between your feelings and the feelings of others, it can become difficult to know exactly whose feelings are whose. With so many possibilities, it is not easy to see which possibility has more value than the others.

This is what happens to visual people trying to get organized. Their brains, so quick to move from one thing to another, so able to see many perspectives, don't stay still long enough to get a single thing done. Organization requires some amount of sequential thinking. You can't simply do everything at once. It doesn't do any good to see these things from every angle. The thinking style that makes someone like Alex so skilled at finding a problem and coming up with a solution leaves him at a loss at ordinary and routine tasks. And Emily doesn't realize that she is involved in so many projects that she moves on to something new before she has finished what she is doing.

When Speed Slows You Down

Many AD/HD, visual thinkers describe their minds as moving quickly from one idea to the next. Usually, these ideas take the form of pictures. Sometimes, people say that their minds resemble a television, quickly changing from channel to channel, and that they do not seem to have control of the remote. If your mind is like this, you might even see a split screen, or a number of different pictures at the same time.

These pictures move so fast that you are unable to use them productively, even if the content of the pictures is important. Ideas and plans make sense but get lost because of the rapidity with which they move. You might even have ideas that are in a useful sequence, but you can't hold onto the ideas long enough to implement them.

Sometimes, you might experience the quick change from one idea to another in the form of distractibility or impulsivity. You start with one task, get reminded of another, and don't stay with the first long enough to do anything useful.

Whether the speed is in the form of rapidly changing thoughts or of rapidly changing ideas, the speed of movement does not result in speed of accomplishment. If you have this kind of thinking you can feel very busy, even get exhausted, but end up getting very little productive work done. Pretty commonly, you start out trying to clean something up or sort something out, but end up with a bigger mess, something more complicated, or something completely unrelated to your initial project.

Ouches Everywhere

Emily thought she was pretty easygoing, compared to her sister, Lisa. Anticipating a weekend visit from her sister, Emily paid even more attention to little details than she usually did. She vacuumed twice: dust made Lisa sneeze. She bought a new air purifier: Lisa was always the one who'd sniff several times, look around, and ask, "Do you smell that?" No one else ever did. Emily put the softest sheets she could find on the bed, because she knew that if she didn't, Lisa would sit at the breakfast table scratching herself from head to toe. She put a fan in the spare bedroom, and low-watt bulbs in the lamps.

If she could keep Lisa physically comfortable, then Lisa might be less irritable than usual. Emily loved Lisa, who was funny and warm and loving. But Lisa got her feelings hurt easily. She was like a mimosa plant, folding up when something brushed by her.

Lisa is like many people with AD/HD. She is extra sensitive to the external world, and to her internal, emotional world. Her sensitivities make her subject to distractions from every direction. She finds herself putting a lot of energy into setting the stage for herself, attempting to tune out as many distractions as possible. Feeling on edge much of the time, often because of subliminal levels of sensory input, she doesn't feel at her best and doesn't work efficiently. And her sensitivity to others leads her to be very self-conscious about her performance. She is very self-critical, and would rather anticipate all possible failures on her part rather than be surprised by them.

People with Lisa's sensitivities spend a lot of time wondering what others think of them. They don't want to hurt others' feelings any more than they want other people to hurt theirs. But, since many people with AD/HD are not very good at reading social cues, this effort doesn't always produce results.

The consequence of all of this sensitivity is a lot of energy going into things that aren't very productive. This doesn't leave enough time and energy to focus on urgent and important matters. And this, of course, interferes in its own way with organization.

Perfectionism

Emily and Alex have a son, Kyle. Like his parents, Kyle tried as hard as he could to do what he was supposed to do. Very much like Emily, he was quite critical of himself, so much so that Emily hated to make comments about his work, even if he asked for her input. The tiniest suggestion that he had made a mistake would set him off.

Kyle's teachers noticed that there were times that he didn't just fail to finish a project. He wouldn't even start it! He spent hours at a time, it seemed, staring at blank pieces of paper. He wouldn't even have the first sentence of a book report written when the other students were correcting their completed first drafts. He would still be trying to decide what country to study when the other students would have gathered materials for their reports. Even his art teacher noticed him sitting at a blank piece of paper or lump of clay, while the other students busily engaged in their projects.

Kyle was a late starter at home, too. He wouldn't try riding a two-wheeler until he was certain he could do it without any difficulty. He yelled at himself when he made any mistake on a computer game. He wouldn't put the books on his bookshelf if he had any doubt about the order in which they belonged. Sometimes, he couldn't even decide what flavor of ice cream to have, though everyone else was almost finished with theirs.

Emily had some of these issues herself. She'd make herself a little bit crazy when she had a dinner party, because she felt the hors d'oeuvres had to coordinate with the main dish—and they had to be homemade, as well. If the napkins that matched the tablecloth had even small stains that she couldn't remove, she'd spend precious hours looking for new ones. No wonder she didn't invite people over all that often. It was way too hard on her!

Visual thinkers usually have a clear and specific picture of how things ought to be. They then want to create a reality to match that picture. The picture they see is, of course, specific and detailed. They expect the reality that they create to match that image. If you are an artist, this is sometimes possible. In fact, many artists do describe simply copying the picture they see in their minds onto the paper or canvas.

But in most other circumstances, making reality perfectly fit a mental picture is pretty much impossible. This makes it difficult for highly visual people to make the transition from what is in their minds to what is in reality. The awareness of the discrepancy between the two can be so clear to them that they don't even want to try. It is so sure to fall short of what they hope to accomplish.

Standard strategies such as "break the task into small bits" don't have much weight, relative to the paralysis and discouragement visual people feel when confronted with a large project. The small bits don't have much relationship to the image in mind. Why work toward such an imperfect goal?

Perfectionism, then, acts as a perpetual drag on the system, often stopping action even before it starts. The clear, picture-perfect image does not reveal its production, from nothing into something, but appears ready-made. There is no instruction sheet, no step-by-step guide for getting from here to there. Without a place to start, and a pathway to get to the finish, it is difficult to start at all.

And the knowledge that the reality may fall far short of the image is discouraging. A poor production is not acceptable in the mind of the perfectionist. The perfect is the enemy of the excellent if nothing at all gets accomplished. Kyle wouldn't ride a bike until he knew he could do it perfectly. He wouldn't draw a picture unless he knew he could make it exactly right. But a blank sheet of paper brought him a score of zero.

When the process does get underway, unbalanced attention to minor details threatens the whole procedure. Emily's focus on the right napkins took time away from pretty much everything in her life, not just from the dinner party. A few stains, unnoticeable to all but those with true obsessive-compulsive problems, are much less important than the food served, or the relaxed atmosphere set by the hostess. Both were threatened by Emily's obsession with perfection.

Adding, in a sense, a huge insult to injury, visual thinkers tend to be more sensitive to everything than others. People with AD/HD are known to be more sensitive and reactive than non-AD/HD people. This sensitivity includes sensitivity to feelings and emotions. Thus, failure, which hurts everyone, hurts visual thinkers more intensely.

No one likes to try and fail. People tend to avoid things that they think will bring failure. But if that failure brings intense pain, then that avoidance enters the realm of the nearly phobic. People not only avoid the things that bring them this kind of pain, they also avoid even thinking about those things.

How, then, does a messy desk, a cluttered bedroom, or an overstuffed garage affect someone with these issues? Those realities are, literally, overwhelming. There is no way to accomplish what needs to be done, no place to start, no visible path from beginning to end. There is no sequence of steps. There is no way to succeed. It is so frustrating and painful to face this kind of task that highly visual people not only don't ever start, sometimes they are even unaware that there is a task to be done.

Time: A Linear Concept

Jane never meant to be late for the movies, and she certainly never meant to let her friends down. She knew what time each movie started. She had a general idea of how long it would take to get from her home to the theater. She knew what she had to do to get herself ready to go. But she could not put all of the pieces together.

Like many people with AD/HD, she held the concept "7:15" in her mind. That was the time that the movie started, and that was the time on which she focused. She had no sense, however, of how to get from where she was, still in her gardening clothes and not having eaten anything since breakfast, to sitting in her seat at the theater, watching the opening credits. That process remained a mystery to her.

For our purposes, rather than those of Albert Einstein, time is a linear concept. There may be nothing as disharmonious for a visual thinker with AD/HD! Time, so emphasized in our culture, is a linear, left-brain concept. It is finite, and defined, and has characteristics such as a beginning, a middle, and an end.

For visual thinkers and many with AD/HD, however, time does not have such clear boundaries. Sometimes, it stretches into infinity.

One thing may connect to another, wrapping around, again and again and coming back on itself like an M. C. Escher drawing. There is no obvious beginning or end.

It is difficult to get an "infinite" AD/HD mind to wrap around a "finite" concept like time. Time feels arbitrary and limiting, and it can be a painful experience for the zestful, entrepreneurial, creative AD/HD spirit. It can disappear into the mental fog of the unfocused, dreamy, inattentive AD/HD state of mind. It is also a royal pain for everybody else dealing with that AD/HD person who is always late. Such behavior feels disrespectful and thoughtless.

What to Do?

The goal in working with these thinking styles is to create a setting in which you can maximize the strength of your style. By understanding how your thinking works, you are much better able to create systems and strategies that work with that style. A vital part of understanding your style is to do everything that you can to help you keep an image in your mind. Anything that you can do to promote that ability will help you stay clear about your goals and will help you stay clear as you move forward.

3

Gaining Control

Your Physical Self

We've talked about AD/HD as a neurological problem, a condition involving purely mental processes. But the body and mind are not separate. How you treat your physical self will have an enormous impact on your mental abilities. If you have AD/HD, you may find that you assume that your high energy is going to carry you through, and that your physical self will take care of itself.

Perhaps you are like Lily, who was pretty sure that she could handle just about anything that came her way. No matter what the circumstances, she would expect herself to rise above them and to do whatever needed to be done. So, when her best friend broke her leg in a skiing accident, Lily took over running the school auction for her, even though she was already behind in running her own busy household.

In order to take on her friend's responsibilities on top of everything that was already on her plate, she had to stretch herself pretty thin. She skipped most of her exercise classes, ate fast food (when she took the time to eat at all), and she kept a schedule that assumed that no stoplights would ever be red, and that her car would never run out of gas. She didn't take the time to drink much water, and started to get dehydrated. In her tension, she often held her breath.

She found herself losing scraps of paper on which she had written important phone numbers. She was late for appointments. At home, she appeared to be listening to her family, though her mind was clearly elsewhere. Exhausted at the end of each day, she couldn't fall asleep, because her mind got more and more active as she tried to remember everything she had to do the following day, and she criticized herself for her failures of the day that had just ended.

She woke up each morning berating herself for being so disorganized. But this state of affairs was inevitable. Possessing an active, intelligent, and resourceful AD/HD brain, she expected herself to perform under any and all circumstances. She had pushed herself many times to achieve, so she was convinced that she could accomplish just about whatever she wanted to accomplish. She knew, just as well, that after each such exertion she would crash in physical and mental exhaustion.

People with AD/HD may be able to throw a fabulous dinner party, teach a brilliant jujitsu class, and do any number of energetic and innovative things. But you probably find that the biggest challenge for you is remembering the basics like brushing your teeth, eating lunch, and even, as in Lily's case, breathing!

AD/HD symptoms vary, depending on the context. Because the preferred context for the AD/HD brain is one with plenty of stimulation, you put a lot more energy into interesting things than into more ordinary but necessary things. Just about anything is more interesting than keeping a regular schedule of sleeping and eating. However, almost nothing will make as big a difference in getting maximum performance from an AD/HD brain as healthy living habits.

As energetic as it may be, the AD/HD brain is not sturdier, but actually is more sensitive than the average brain. In order to function well, it has to be treated well. When stressed, performance suffers. Yet the majority of people with AD/HD push themselves as Lily does, ignoring healthy activities such as physical activity and appropriate relaxation, as well as the basic tasks of daily living like getting enough sleep and eating regularly.

Underlying the program we present for learning to focus your visually gifted mind in order to organize your life are the fundamentals of taking care of your body.

Establish a regular sleep/wake cycle. One of the special (and, often, guilty) pleasures of many people with AD/HD is staying up late at night, when everyone else is asleep. Somehow, the energy to really focus seems to surge just when it is time to wind down for the day and go to sleep. After long periods of feeling scattered, unfocused, or at loose ends, that delicious sense of purpose that comes late at night seems irresistible.

It is much more easily said than done, but you must learn to resist the urge to stay up late at night. In fact, this may turn out to be the biggest single challenge for you in getting a more organized life. There is no magic answer for giving up those late nights. We'll make a few suggestions, but it will be up to you to find what works for you. And, just to put this in context, Joan spends more time talking with her patients about the need for adequate, restful sleep than any other single subject!

As a realistic bedtime approaches, it might help you to jot down a few notes, so that you don't forget the latest brilliant idea that pops into your mind right at 11:00 p.m. Write only enough to be able to identify the subject. Don't elaborate.

Determine to be productive the next day. Think about how much better you will feel. If you stay up late and have to get up early, you will be sleep-deprived the next day. And it is very, very clear that sleep deprivation mimics the symptoms of AD/HD. It is also clear that if you sleep late in order to catch up on your sleep, and then get up early the next day, you have basically created the equivalent of jet lag. If you decide to sleep in on the weekend, then you're not going to be at your best when you get up at your regular time on Monday.

Enlist the help of your family or anyone you live with or sleep with. Tell them that your goal is to get to bed on time, and ask them to encourage you in this goal. Do this with appreciation and kindness. Do not punish them for doing what you have asked.

Set up small steps. If your usual bedtime has been 2:00 a.m., then move that back to 1:45 for a week, then 1:30, and so on.

Learn about "sleep hygiene," the medical term for good sleep habits. These are simple things like reducing stimulation, getting distractions out of the bedroom and avoiding exercise right before going to bed. You may find strategies in this area that are new to you and that will help.

Some people find that their favorite time is early in the morning, again, when the rest of the world is asleep and there are no distractions. There is nothing wrong with getting up early and doing your work while you mind is fresh. But if you stay up late and then get up early, you start to cut into your required sleep. People who do this often find that they do fine in the beginning of the day but fade seriously in the afternoon. If you do this, you will then suffer from all of the same problems associated with sleep deprivation. And you create a sort of vicious cycle. Unable to function well in the second part of your day because of your fatigue, you have the idea that only getting up extra early will help you catch up.

Keep in mind that part of the difficulty with AD/HD is that your mind is not always alert when you want it to be, and it doesn't always want to sleep when you want it to. A regular sleep/wake schedule will not fix that problem, but there is no doubt that it will help.

Eat a healthy, well-balanced diet. We recognize that telling you what to eat can be overwhelming, confusing, and even intrusive. But there are some simple recommendations that will make a huge difference in your physical and mental energy.

Plenty of protein, especially in the morning, will help you maintain your blood glucose, and as a result, clarity of thinking. Protein provides amino acids, important building blocks for all of those neurotransmitters we have been talking about.

Avoiding sugary and refined foods will also help stabilize your blood sugar and will slow the depletion of important nutrients. The craving for carbohydrates and sugary foods is often a result of low energy. You know that if you have that doughnut and coffee, you will have a burst of energy. It happens to be a short-lived burst, followed by another crash, and another craving for a quick fix. This habit is common, understandable, and happens to everybody from time to time. It seems hard to change, but a few days of focusing on protein intake will help you break the cycle more quickly than you might think.

Each person has his or her own individual dietary needs, and many people know what helps them function better. When you discover this, make use of it, rather than assume that what you eat doesn't matter.

Because of the tendency to hyperfocus, many people with AD/HD can get so absorbed in something interesting that they forget to eat. If this happens to you, when you forget to eat you probably don't even feel hungry. It's as if you don't need food at times like this, because the stimulation seems to fulfill your hunger. This is, however, an illusion. You may get away with skipping food for a short time, but if you skip meals, your performance will suffer.

Get regular exercise. Perhaps you tend to be moody or feel depressed or unmotivated. You may have dips in your energy, especially in the early afternoon. Maybe you find yourself obsessively worrying. All of these things interfere with focus and concentration. None of them can be "cured" but all of them can be improved with regular, and especially, vigorous exercise. Boosts in serotonin and endorphins (which improve mood), stabilization of blood sugar, and overall well-being are proven benefits of moving your body.

For some people this is easy, because some kind of sports activity is a part of who they are. For others, this is one of those burdensome "shoulds" that nag at them. If you are of the first type, keep on enjoying what you do. Everything else you aim for will be easier because you keep moving your body. Many people with AD/HD need to move in order to think. If this is how you are, then exercise is crucial for you.

If you are one who has trouble with exercise programs, our best advice is to find something fun to do. Play your favorite music and dance around the living room. Go for a walk with a friend, a run or Frisbee game with your dog, or shoot a few baskets. Like most people you may do better in a class, where the energy from others is contagious and the peer pressure keeps you from quitting just because you're a little out of breath or your calves ache.

It also helps to set small, attainable goals, and gradually work your way toward regular activity. Five minutes of walking is better than no minutes. Every set of stairs you take instead of the elevator will help you. Walking down stairs is just as good as walking up, and has its own health benefits.

Your Physical Space

For most of you, this is the last frontier. This is the Mount Everest of your organizational challenges: your *stuff*. It is a vast territory of chaos and clutter, worthy of a modern-day Lewis and Clark. The scope of the problem is the product of both your disorganization and your active, creative mind. Many books and many experts have useful suggestions for conquering the clutter, and if you take advantage of them, you are likely to find strategies that can help you. Because that territory is so well covered elsewhere, we are not going to spend time on those specifics.

There is one specific aspect of clutter that is especially relevant to the program. We are going to give you a simple, day-by-day program that will work to harness and strengthen your visual skills. We will be asking you to close your eyes during your visualization exercises, because what you see in your immediate environment will distract you.

All that we are going to ask you to do for this program is to clear one small space. Please resist the temptation to use this as a starting point for the great clean-out that you have been promising yourself for years. The purpose of the small step that you will take at the beginning of the program is to create a space for you to use for clearing and calming your mind so that you can focus on the simple visualization exercises.

The Angle on Angles

Most people with this visual type of thinking consider it to be one of their most valuable gifts. It truly is a gift. Having a view of many different angles at once is an asset in many settings. The more a person can do this, the more potential they have to create extremely vivid and memorable images.

Most people do the best they can, most of the time. The person making the best use of this thinking style, then, often ends up being a creative, but disorganized, or erratic or sometimes immature person. However, the deficits that are so obvious in this description are pretty negative characteristics of a mature, successful adult. Protecting themselves from the shame and self-criticism, many people with this set of characteristics just consider themselves to be relaxed or casual or not hung up on unimportant details. They may see other people as overly picky or controlling. They may not come to grips with their own difficulties. And they therefore do not see that any intervention is necessary.

But if this kind of thinking style isn't managed, then disorganization, fragmentation, and failure often result. Lots of projects are conceived, few get implemented. Lots of projects get started, but few finished. The truth is that if the angle of view keeps moving, that's when you have a problem. The issue that pretty much determines when this gift becomes a problem is whether or not you can keep your view on one angle at a time, long enough to create a mental image that you can use for planning and remembering your goals.

And, as much as creative people hate to admit it, this is a problem. Just admitting it can sometimes be key to improved functioning, because this gives a person the possibility of thinking of things from one angle at a time. But, difficult as it is for people who so highly prize this aspect of themselves, this moving view is often a part of visual thinking that requires medical intervention in order to gain substantial improvement.

All of the health-related issues we discussed earlier in this chapter can be tried before medication is used. Regular sleep is probably the single most helpful lifestyle habit that can help give a person the mental strength to harness this kind of thinking. Vigorous daily exercise can be dramatic in both promoting more sound and restful sleep as well as in calming the mind for hours at a time.

But, as many psychiatrists say when trying to help a person accept that medication might be appropriate for them, there is no shame in not being able to change symptoms through sheer willpower. If you had insulin-dependent diabetes, you would not expect to lower your blood sugar by wishing and hoping. Sometimes, all the mental work in the world is not enough to keep the mind on track. A psychiatric consultation and trial of medication might really be of benefit.

Slowing Down from Fast-Forward

Rapid-fire thinking is great in a crisis, but doesn't let you stick with a mental image long enough to make it real and effective. When we talked about how to deal with seeing many angles at once, we discussed the need to stick with one angle. When it comes to rapid-fire thinking, you have to be able to stop your mental images from moving if you want to become more clear, organized, and focused. You have to be able to attend to things long enough to get them fully into your memory for later use.

The same types of interventions apply here as for seeing things from many different angles. Anything that promotes steady, healthy overall functioning will help you gain control of your thoughts. Of course, this is sort of paradoxical for fast-paced people. All that organization and regularity is not only boring, it is downright painful. The exuberance that many rapid-fire thinkers also demonstrate in their physical lives is a force that is difficult to stop.

It's not impossible to have some impact on it. The most immediate remedy for going too fast is something everyone can do: *breathe*. Though the default position for AD/HD is "go," you still need to stop. A few deep breaths can get you centered in just seconds. Slow your breathing down. Breathe in for the count of four, then out for the count of four. See if, in a few breaths, you can slow it down to the count of eight.

Rapid thinking is another aspect of AD/HD and right-brain thinking in which medications might be crucial. If you cannot slow your mind down enough to make a clear picture that you can later retrieve, you will not be able to have access to all of your thoughts, learning, and creativity.

If this is the case, you should seriously consider adding some professional help to your plans. True, without therapy or medication, there will be times that you can focus, concentrate, and organize. The question is, can you do it enough, and can you do it when you need to? If you can't, and therefore cannot depend on having those times of focus and organization, there will probably be very little organization in your life. If you don't have some ability to access your skills when you need them, you will continue to be at the whim of your circumstances and preferences. There will be no predictability and, therefore, almost by definition, no organization.

Medication

Most people who take medication for AD/HD do so with some conflict. Most people have tried everything else they can do and turn to medication as a last resort. Many people, however, are optimistic and hopeful that something is finally going to help them in their struggles.

We want you to know that although medications can be incredibly helpful, and are a vital part of the overall management for most people with AD/HD, they do not work best by themselves. They level the playing field considerably, and they solve many problems. But they do not replace, as boring as this sounds, healthy living habits. They also do not substitute for knowing how your mind works, understanding its strengths and weaknesses, and adjusting your life accordingly.

Many people do not have access to or choose not to see a psychiatrist with special training in treating AD/HD. Sadly, though as common in adults as conditions such as anxiety and depression, there are still not enough psychiatrists familiar enough with the condition and its treatment. This is because, until recently, it was assumed that AD/HD went away after childhood. We now know that it simply goes underground.

However, there is no one single pattern of AD/HD and there is no one size that fits all. If you choose to use medication, it needs to be individualized to your specific symptoms and reactions to medication. Your overall physical condition should be included in the evaluation, including sleep patterns, diet, physical activity, use of stimulants such as caffeine, and use of tobacco and other drugs. Chronic illnesses should be noted and other medications that you are taking evaluated. Thyroid and other hormonal conditions should be screened for.

In the appendix, we provide an overview of specific medications, the pros and cons of each, and their common side effects. For now, it helps to be aware of what it is about your AD/HD that you want to change with medications. You will want to have a short list of target symptoms that you will be able to use as measures for improvement.

You may be very excited about what medication can do for you. But be aware that there is usually some grieving to do. There is some disappointment in recognizing that what you see as some of the most wonderful things about you are also slowing you down and limiting you in your life. Grieving that loss can be so painful that you avoid it and, along with it, avoid addressing the need to do things differently for yourself and in your life. There is no change, though, without loss. If you need a little counseling (or a lot of counseling) to help you accept these realities, so be it. Denying reality leaves it forever unchanged. Grieving reality, however, is actually a process of movement and growth, and allows for creativity and change.

The Princess (or Prince) and the Pea

Extra sensitivity is a part of the creativity and connectedness of many people with AD/HD and visual thinking. Some of this sensitivity turns out to take quite a lot of management. It makes you one of those "high-maintenance" people. In order to function well or to feel okay, the lights have to be a certain way. It can't be too noisy or too quiet. There can't be any buzzing of the refrigerator. The neighbors can't be barbecuing.

You might be so used to this characteristic way of experiencing the world that you don't realize that everybody doesn't have it. But they don't. If they were to tell you the truth, it's likely that they might find you a bit of a pain in the neck, to be polite. They most likely find your needs strange or annoying. And they certainly don't understand what the big deal is about all these things.

And they really don't understand how much energy it takes for you to manage your sensitivities. Chances are that you are so used to managing yourself that you don't even realize what an energy drain this process can be. Other people might find you to be high maintenance for them. The person for whom you are most high maintenance, however, is yourself.

As with the other characteristics of right-brained visual thinkers, this tendency is not negative in itself. But when it uses up too much energy, it doesn't allow you to go forward with creating and achieving plans. And anyone who has been unable to concentrate because of the sound of hammering or a boom box knows that cognitive strength is drained when the physical environment is too disruptive.

Right-brain sensitivities, as we have said, also include emotional sensitivities. Taking things too much to heart, worrying about what other people think, or obsessing about emotional disruptions are other large energy drains. Putting yourself in another person's shoes is the basic requirement for empathy. But when you put yourself in someone else's shoes and get lost there and forget to come back to your own, you've lost yourself in someone else's feelings.

Many people with AD/HD pick up on a lot of nonverbal communication. They read subtle body language as well as pick up on unexpressed emotion. However, many people with AD/HD are not particularly articulate in the language of social cues. They don't accurately assess the raw data that they absorb. The emotional information they are working with, then, is often misinterpreted and is therefore inaccurate. Learning to understand better what is coming in, and at least to be suspicious of emotional judgments, can be a big energy saver.

It makes sense to do all that you can to limit the information that you are dealing with so that you can work most efficiently with what you have. Setting aside a quiet place at home, or finding a quiet place at school or the office is important. Some people need music or white noise in order to concentrate. Do what you can to set up the environment to be as helpful to you as you can. You may need noise-filtering headphones. You may need to work on the lighting in your home or at work. Remove the distractions over which you have control. This includes relationships. Don't start asking your significant other why they did something you don't like right before you have to start a difficult project.

Get vigorous physical exercise. This helps with sensory processing and helps even out distracting physical and emotional irritations. And, as with other aspects of the AD/HD brain, sometimes medications can help even out emotions and distracting thoughts.

When the Perfect Is the Enemy of the Excellent

Add the sensitivity and extra awareness of the visual thinker to the perfectionism of someone who can create a perfect picture in their mind's eye, and you have a recipe for procrastination. The real task is one of basic cognitive reframing. There is a belief that not doing something perfectly is going to feel so awful that it will be intolerable. Ironically, this fear of failure for lack of perfection is superimposed on someone who has a pretty good record of failure over ordinary simple things. Why even try?

As with basic cognitive and behavioral therapy, there are two parts to getting past this roadblock. One is the self-talk you engage in. This needs to change to reframe the goal from perfect to excellent. And sometimes, even "good" is good enough!

The other is basic desensitization. This is taking on the thing you are avoiding a little bit at a time, so that you can tolerate it. You have to practice a little bit each day in doing something you ordinarily wouldn't try. Make it a relatively small thing that is not likely to literally crush you. Then check your reaction. Breathe. Live with it. Realize that it didn't kill you. Continue to try a little bit at a time to do things that might lead to your definition of failure (that is, lack of perfection). As you are able to tolerate more and more small bits of this discomfort, you will break down the intensity of resistance to trying new things.

Creating Rewards

As you work through the program, you will be asked to take small steps to attain your ultimate goal. We know that when you have an image of what you want, it is hard not to have it show up immediately. The small steps can be so disappointing and boring that you don't have motivation to move on. This is why rewards are important for you. As we have said, many of the tasks in and of themselves are not rewards. Even the successful completion of them is not enough. You need something to work for that is pleasurable to you. You need something to look forward to at each stage of your progress.

You need to have those rewards available at the moment that you complete the task. You don't want to find yourself having completed a difficult day or week of this program wondering what you will do to reward yourself. You want to have that reward in mind as you do the hard work. So you need to create the rewards before you get started.

You will want to have some specific rewards of various sizes.

These should not be the most ordinary things. They should be treats. They are very personal. If you have a hobby, it might be a particular item that you've been wanting but couldn't really justify. If you like food, it can be a specific gourmet item or meal. Perhaps you will get yourself a bottle of fine wine.

Maybe it's services you want. It might be a pedicure, a massage, or a new haircut.

Maybe it's a new lipstick or perfume.

Maybe it's a CD or special tech gadget.

Make yourself a little list of special treats that you will aim for as you work your way through the program. Enjoy planning this. You're going to do some work, and we want you to enjoy yourself along the way.

A Reality Check

Though there are lots of strategies, interventions, and techniques that help promote organizational competence in people with AD/HD and visual thinking, the truth is that if you are one of these people, it is likely that you never will be the picture of organization. Your strengths lie in other areas. Yes, you can reduce difficulties. But it is most important to know yourself, to recognize who you are, with the limitations that go with your reality. With that knowledge you can make the most of who you are, and you can stop banging your head against the wall by trying to be something that you are not.

This process of knowing yourself entails facing two things about yourself. These can be so difficult to face alone that some psychotherapy can be helpful here. First of all, part of getting clear on who you are involves identifying your strengths, not just your weaknesses. People who have felt criticized, who have felt like failures, and who feel like frauds whenever they achieve something good have a very difficult time getting clear on what is good about themselves.

The other difficult aspect is that truly acknowledging areas of deficit involves some grieving. There is loss in recognizing what you wish you could do but cannot do. There is loss in seeing how you have struggled unnecessarily over the years. There isn't any way to become clear about who you really are without experiencing some loss. In order to avoid that pain, many people never really get to the truth, and therefore miss the opportunities that could open up for them. The good news about grieving, and the reason to push through it, is that it is a normal, natural, and time-limited process. It allows you to let go and move forward.

4

Tricks of the Memory Trade

Finishing with the Phobia

The simplest things sometimes seem out of reach. If these things were complicated, it would make sense to put them off forever. But they aren't. And, yet, some of us treat them as if we are facing a session of bamboo spikes under the fingernails. Perhaps we are a bit like Ed, caught in the same spot again.

Ed sat at his desk, staring at the usual disaster. Stacks, some six or eight inches high, perched and balanced on each other and covered almost the entire writing surface. Sound familiar? But, as it is with many people who use this "horizontal filing system," Ed felt confident that he knew what was in each of the piles. It was a good thing that he did, because he had two bills that had to be paid immediately. If he didn't get the payment made by the end of the banking day, he would incur eighty-six dollars in late fees, and it was most likely that his cell phone would not be working by the weekend.

It would take only seconds to locate the bills that Ed had to pay.

But Ed sat and stared at his desk. "I should do this," ran through his thoughts, and yet his body didn't move. What was it that made it so difficult for him to get this small chore over with? He looked at his watch. He had just under half an hour to get the bills to the mailbox two blocks away. Suddenly galvanized into activity, he dug furiously through the piles. In minutes, he had the bills he needed, a checkbook, and a pen. Now that he had the checks written (though not entered into the register) and the envelopes sealed, all he had to do was find some stamps. Scrounging through his top drawer, he found three. Wow, and he only needed two! He bounded out of the front door, jogged three blocks, and dropped the bills into the mailbox with minutes to spare.

Ambling home, feeling a mellow feeling of relief and calm, Ed asked himself a question that most people with AD/HD ask of themselves quite regularly: "That wasn't so bad. Why didn't I get that started earlier?" Although this is asked as a rhetorical question, there is a very good answer. The stimulation created by the deadline creates enough dopamine to get the odious task done. It's as simple as that. This is one of the ways in which medication is often helpful, because it raises the level of dopamine enough to get started and to complete the job. But there's more to this than just a need for medication.

For everyone with AD/HD, there will always be tasks so boring, so tedious, so painful, that they get put off as long as possible. Medicine is part of the solution. But there have to be other tricks that make difficult tasks easier to start and to complete.

We use the word "trick" intentionally, because often what works is to rearrange things to make them look different. We trick ourselves, in a way, into thinking they are something different. By doing that, we can leapfrog over one of the biggest roadblocks to getting more focused and organized when it comes to difficult tasks: bad memories.

When you have repeated bad experiences doing difficult things, even if you have pretty effective neurochemistry, even if you have learned new skills, even if you have a clear understanding of your problem, you still have the buildup of years of experiencing failure and pain. Every time you think of one of those difficult things, even if it is just at the edge of your awareness, you relive the negative feelings. Naturally, then, you want to avoid that situation.

Linda Lewis, LCSW, an expert in the psychotherapy of AD/HD, suggests that the association of negative feelings and memories with the automatic avoidance of those situations creates an almost phobic reaction. This is not the same thing as, say, a phobia about snakes or high places. Those are true phobias, with overt symptoms of panic in the face of a particular situation or stimulus. But the end result is very similar: an automatic avoidance of that situation because of the negative feelings associated with it.

So the trick is to transform one thing into another. Then it does not trigger the same "phobic" reaction, with its attendant avoidance and procrastination. If we can create a different set of associations or meanings, we can change the thing into something else.

Standard treatment for a phobia involves desensitization, a procedure in which a person is exposed to very small portions of the thing that causes the phobic reaction. If the portions are small enough, they will not trigger a full reaction, and the person learns to tolerate a manageable amount of the bad feeling. The portions are increased, a little bit at a time, until the person can tolerate the actual thing without having an extreme reaction.

There are other things we can do, however, that take advantage of the reality of who you are. We want, whenever possible, to build on your strengths.

Accentuate the Positive

Ed was finally able to solve his acute bill-paying problem in a way that many people with stronger left-brain abilities would not be able to manage. He was able to see the specific immediate need, to dive right in, to deal only with what was absolutely necessary, and to get it done on time. In this particular case, you could argue that we are making necessity a virtue. You would be correct. And that is not necessarily a bad thing, because we want to be able to look at the skills that Ed does possess, so that he can use them to make up for the skills that he lacks.

Remember that the brain usually creates a pathway to accomplish necessary things. That pathway, as we know, varies among individuals. We also know that when one avenue is closed, another one opens up. Ed's difficulty in addressing tasks that require slow, steady, methodical activity is in some way balanced by his ability to cut to the chase and quickly accomplish what he needs to do.

Organizational experts offer strategies that are useful to a broad range of people. A number of them offer specific help to people with AD/HD and visual learning styles, because they do capitalize on their strengths. Some work best for linear, left-brained thinkers. As you try different strategies and find what works for you, you may find that you end up using those techniques that maximize your strengths, rather than forcing yourself to focus on your weaknesses. Ed has an ability to do things quickly. This is likely to be a strategy that he can use to his advantage.

Breaking Up Is Easy to Do

How hard is it to hang up one shirt, to fold one towel, to get some postage stamps, to look through one stack of papers for a bill, or to make one phone call? None of these single tasks is particularly difficult. But how hard is it to put away all the clothes that you have dropped on the floor and hung on chairs and laid on the bed? Or how hard is it to gather paper, envelopes, checkbook, pen, and all your bills? Or how hard is it to wash, dry, and fold two loads of laundry? Or how hard is it to clear and sort what is on your entire desk? Obviously, these are much, much harder.

Large, multistepped tasks are typically more likely to produce an avoidant reaction. They require a large amount of mental energy. They cannot be dispatched quickly with a simple, quick, or automatic action.

It doesn't take much to get the paper if you have it delivered daily. You open the front door and pick it up, or you throw on your slippers and run out to the driveway. The task doesn't require much thought, planning, or sequencing. It's such a quick, automatic activity that many people don't even bother putting on their slippers.

But how does everything change if you have to go to the store to buy the paper? Now you might have a whole different story. Maybe in addition to the paper, you also need to pick up a few things. But to do that, you'll have to make a list. You don't know if you need eggs or milk, and it's hard to check on the eggs because you had a party last night and the leftovers are all on the shelf in front of the eggs and you'd have to move them all to find them. You don't know if you should wake up your wife to ask her if there is something she wants you to pick up while you are there. Now, getting the paper has become a more complex procedure. You might end up just eating a piece of cold pizza and checking the Internet for the news and weather and hoping that your wife will get up soon and decide she wants to go get the paper herself.

It's easy to call your brother just to say "hi" and talk about the great movie you saw last night or the game coming up in the afternoon. You two always have a lot of laughs and so you look forward to those phone calls.

But what if you need to figure out when you are going to go together to visit your parents? You have to have your calendar in front of you. You have to know when your vacation time is, coordinate that with the times that work for your parents and for your brother, make sure that there are no required school functions for your daughter or sports activities for your son that you have promised not to miss. You have to decide how much time you will spend with your family, and how much vacation time you will have left to spend with your family based on that decision. There are a lot of different pieces of information to hold in mind at one time. One decision depends on another, and some decisions depend on other people, and they all affect other people. This is not something you look forward to.

This turns out to be a huge amount of mental work for a visual thinker with AD/HD. You have to listen, remember, decide, propose, consider, compromise, and plan. All of these require holding a number of thoughts or pieces of data in mind, going back and forth between them, and making decisions based on preferences, cause and effect, and priorities. They take a lot of focus and concentration, they require a very well-functioning active working memory, and they're tiring. There always will be something to avoid or put off.

One of the best strategies for managing these problems is to break them up into much smaller pieces. Each piece should be small enough to represent one simple task or decision. Each individual piece, then, does not require all that mental energy that more complex tasks require. Each individual piece usually will not set off a "phobic," avoidant reaction.

A Collection of Accomplishments

Breaking tasks up into smaller bits is a skill worth developing. When you take each part of a task and redefine it as a self-contained activity, you create many experiences that make everything easier: these are the experiences of success. Each step that you finish is a completed, successful step. There is nothing like the experience of success to reinforce and encourage a behavior. And having that positive experience of success where a person usually experiences failure can start a shift away from the automatic avoidance of those tasks.

Before you can begin to learn to do this, you have to be able to see that large tasks are, in fact, groups of smaller ones. Because you might see one big blur, you might need some help, initially, from someone who can look objectively at your problem. You might not know where to start or how to go about dividing things up. This process of breaking large tasks into smaller segments is often what personal coaches teach people to do.

If you're on your own, there are different ways to start breaking tasks down. On a general level, you can break activities down into three main categories: gathering your materials, using those materials, and putting the materials away. (That last part is actually a step.) Then look at the large, middle section. Perhaps you have a stack of bills to pay. You could break the task down into two or three bills at a time. You stop each part after it is finished, and count it as completed. Get up. Take a break. Pay close attention to your success and enjoy the feeling of having done what you said you were going to do, and then begin another small part. You may be used to downplaying small steps as part of your expectation of failure. But that clearly is not productive. It is much more useful in propelling you along to recognize your small steps and to feel good about them.

If you are trying to do something like plan a family trip that will require a lot of thought and decision making, you can break it up into more individual parts than you might think. For example, you could call your brother and ask what dates he is thinking about. That is the whole task. Don't pursue any additional information, don't try to think about how that will fit into your plans. Just find out what dates he has in mind. Then stop. Finish up with a general conversation. Then, come back to the problem the next day and look at the next question.

Each of these steps is manageable and is not overwhelming. You can do them and get them over with. This brings us to another discussion of time.

Another way to break up tasks is to break them up into bits of time. The bits of time should be individualized to your optimal attention span. If you can concentrate on something for a maximum of fifteen minutes, then break things into pieces of fifteen minutes each. When the time is up, stop.

We are going to repeat ourselves. *When the time is up, stop.*

You may want to keep going, because things are going well. But if your real optimal concentration time is fifteen minutes and you go much further than that, you can expect to find yourself going downhill quickly. The task becomes difficult, you notice yourself daydreaming or losing your effectiveness. The risk here is that you will fall back into old habits and get back into the state in which these things are very difficult. If so, you have lost the opportunity to have a completed, successful task. So set yourself a five or ten minute break, then go for another fifteen minutes.

How many of these individual periods of performance can you manage in a day? The big-thinking perfectionist in you will expect yourself to go on indefinitely. We highly encourage you *not* to do this. A short time of peak performance will be a lot better than a whole day of dragging through your task.

Each of these short segments is an accomplishment in itself. Add them up, and you will see real success. Instead of these dreadful things taking huge amounts of your precious time, they take very little time at all. That's because each one, each part of the task is, in itself, very short.

You will probably find, when you're working only during peak focus times, that you can do these things pretty quickly. And this brings us to the next trick.

Do It Fast

Ed spent weeks worrying about the bills that he had to pay. He spent many hours consciously aware of his need to put those payments in the mail. He spent a total of seventeen minutes actually doing the job, and that included the time it took to walk to the mailbox and back!

It's that speed of performance that we want to harness. Yes, in the emergency phase, it's propelled by sheer adrenaline. But you can still use speed as a tool to get yourself to accomplish things. When you know in a clear and concrete way that something is only going to take a short amount of time, you can work to reduce the anticipatory dread. You are only committing yourself to a few minutes of pain. It's like removing an adhesive bandage. You can pull it off hair by hair and drag out the misery, or you can just yank it off and drastically reduce the discomfort.

To get yourself to do things fast, you will need to build a little history for yourself. Begin by estimating the amount of time it will take to do something at your most efficient. Then set a timer, or visualize the time on your watch or the clock on the wall. Make sure you have a way to keep track. Then, ready, set, go! And when the time is up, whether or not you have finished, stop.

Take a break. Evaluate what you have accomplished. Estimate the shortest amount of time it will take to finish the project. Go!

We know that rapid-fire thinking has its disadvantages. It can be difficult to stay on one subject when too many ideas come into your mind at one time. If acted upon without thinking, rapid-fire thinking becomes impulsivity. A state of anxiety can grow out of rapid thoughts that turn into worries.

But, the same mental processes that lead to rapid-fire thinking can be harnessed to lead to rapid-fire action. What you need to make that work is to have confidence in this ability, and then use that knowledge to gain control of your overall plan and goal. Then you can use your ability to whip through something quickly to get past your roadblocks.

So, using this strength entails two things. The first is to learn to identify when that skill is useful and when it is not. The second is to use your visual skills to clarify your goals before you start.

It is clear that there are times when it makes sense for a visual, right-brained person to slow down his or her thinking, and there are times when it makes sense to speed it up. Slowing down is important when you are taking in information. This is the situation in which you must make a visual image in your mind as you are gathering information from any source in order to store and thus retain that information. The only way to do that effectively is to allow enough time to work with the information in a relaxed, rather than in a rushed, manner. And, as we have said so many times, the more vivid the image that you create, the more effective the memory will be.

The same need to slow your thinking applies to planning and setting a goal for accomplishing any particular task. Before you start a task, make sure you have a vivid image in your mind of what you plan to accomplish. Be sure that the image you create includes the wonderful feeling you will have when you have accomplished your goal. Feel the glow and the satisfaction you will have on an emotional level. You should do this in a slow, relaxed manner, as you do with all of your active visualizations. This is the part of the activity in which it is most important that you slow down your natural rapid-fire thinking.

But, once you have the image in mind, then you can unleash your more zestful side! The ability to do things quickly is an advantage in an emergency. It is useful when you are in a brainstorming or a problem-solving setting, when it helps to be able to consider a lot of different possibilities in a short amount of time. And it is useful for when you have set up a limited, specific, well-defined, and well-visualized task.

For each of these tasks, set your time for getting it done, and just go for it!

Find It a Home

One of the more frustrating aspects of trying to get organized is that your best effort, your real commitment to doing things differently, still doesn't seem to pay off. We want you to remember that what is important is the process, rather than the product. Then use your experience to troubleshoot.

Al was about to face that challenge. He had gotten ready in plenty of time for his 7:00 a.m. appointment. Relaxed and confident, he went to his desk to get his appointment book, but it wasn't there. He wasn't worried, because he'd had this kind of problem before, and he thought he'd find his book. There were a limited number of places where his book could be. He looked on the hall table, and then he looked on the counter between the kitchen and breakfast nook. No luck. He went back to the bedroom, hoping he had left it on his night table. Again, he came up empty.

By now, he was starting to sweat a little. He was starting to run late, despite his strongly held value to always be on time. He began muttering to himself. "I promised myself I was going to leave my book in the same place every day." Clearly, he hadn't. Finally, he figured that he had probably left his book in the car, and he left for his meeting.

The appointment book was not in his car. At the end of the day, when he arrived home, Al continued to look for his book. Finally, once again thinking that he had really lost his book, he sat down at his desk to try to recreate his schedule. He reached for some paper in his vertical files. There, staring at him, was his appointment book.

"What a great place for it," he thought, as he laughed at himself. "I put it here so it would be easy to see."

What Al did not understand about himself was that, as logical as his decision had seemed to him to place his appointment book where he could see it when he was sitting at his desk, it was not a decision based on any organizational principles. It was actually an impulsive decision, made at the spur of the moment. He had been sitting at the desk, and at that moment, he thought a good place for his appointment book was in front of his vertical desk file organizer. He didn't pause and think about it, he didn't create a picture of it in his mind, and he did not visualize himself calmly going to that place when he needed his appointment book. The next time he needed it, then, he could not retrieve a memory of where he had placed it, because he literally had no memory of it.

When he does decide on a place to keep his appointment book, what is most important is that he slow down his thinking, and create a clear and active visual picture of it in his mind. The actual place doesn't matter very much. It could be in his office, in his bedroom, on the stairs leading down to the garage, or on his nightstand. It could be in the refrigerator! (Many of you, we know, have found things like appointment books and telephones that you have absentmindedly left in the vegetable bin.) What matters is that Al put in the focus and time to create a picture of it in his mind.

Professional organizers always say that to organize your things, everything must have a "home." Left-brained thinkers, who naturally gravitate toward the organizational field, have no difficulty finding that home. And they have no difficulty using that home on a regular basis to keep their things, their projects, and their time in the places where they belong.

But it is different for right-brained thinkers. Like Al, they put stuff down based on their immediate need, rather than based on a sequence of needs. The immediate need is to move on from the current situation and on to the next. This might mean leaving the milk out on the counter all day, leaving the phone on the windowsill, leaving clothes on the floor, and leaving the keys on the floor next to the couch. Everything has a home everywhere!

For right-brained thinkers, finding a home for something does require the same slow, relaxed process that allows the person to actively visualize in order to choose a good home and to lock that into memory. And it is important to add the feeling of satisfaction that goes with having things where they belong.

There is no fast or simple way to accomplish this. It is going to be more difficult for right-brained thinkers to do this than it is for left-brained thinkers. But the organizing specialists are correct in the importance of finding everything a home. The tendency for right-brained people, of course, is to have a vision of perfect organization and to think that they should achieve that. But, as we have said, it is important to break things into small pieces. And so it is important to remember that you don't have to find a home for everything in one day. Each step is a true accomplishment.

The homes you pick need to work for you. Your choices will not be the same as those of left-brained, natural organizers. Most visual thinkers do not use files very well if those files are hidden in a drawer. Those files might need to be more visible. Baskets, boxes, and shelves that are clearly visible work better for visual thinkers. This is an area in which organizers who work with AD/HD people have very worthwhile suggestions.

The bigger challenge, after each thing has a home, is to use it. Ready to move on to the next thing before they have finished what they are doing, right-brained thinkers do not naturally enjoy the process of returning each thing to its home. Anything you can do to make this fun is going to be helpful. A whimsical coat rack may be better for you than a subdued one. A colorful basket for your bills might be better than a plain wooden box. But, again, this step requires a slowing down process. There is no magic answer. We are giving you the same advice here as in many other areas. You do need to learn to stop, think, and picture the benefits of keeping things in order. As you work with this process, rewarding yourself for your accomplishment makes a lot of sense.

Find a Friend

Many of the organizational difficulties for people with AD/HD start early in life. Perhaps you have had some experiences that are a lot like Kelly's.

Kelly brought home her report card, dreading the usual questions, accusations, and predictions. "If you would just do your homework, don't you think you could get better than a D in science?" pushed her father. "Besides, you used to love science." It was a question, but she knew her father didn't really want an answer.

From the other side of the room came the familiar, "You could do it if you really wanted to!" Her mother was right about that. But Kelly didn't always want to. "If you keep this up, you'll never succeed at anything!" That one always got her, because that one seemed real. She didn't know how she ever would be successful in life if school was this difficult.

Kelly's parents didn't buy her explanations, so she didn't give them anymore. But her actions did have explanations. Her science teacher was mean and sneering and he didn't really like kids. It felt icky in his classroom, and it made it hard for her to put herself into her work. And the Spanish teacher was just disorganized and boring. Spanish class consisted of nothing but memorizing, and it wasn't interesting at all.

It had always been like this for Kelly. If she liked her teacher, she did well in that class. In fact, she could be an exceptional student. But if she didn't much like the teacher, and if, for some reason, the teacher didn't like her, then passing the class at all was an achievement. She just couldn't make herself do it.

You probably remember the same sort of thing. When someone inspired you or tapped into your imagination, you would soak up information like a sponge. If they thought you were special, you'd do anything for them. You'd get energy from being around them, and you'd do things you never knew you could. But someone you don't respect can't get you to do much of anything. And if they are regularly critical of you, your energy just evaporates. You can't perform at all.

So, you have experienced early in life how relationships with, and feelings from and for and about other people, dramatically affect your performance. You can take advantage of this by finding ways to use other people to help you stay focused and to follow through on tasks.

Experts in coaching people with AD/HD often suggest using other people to help accomplish what is most difficult. Just having another person with you can make a huge difference. They may or may not help you in concrete, practical ways. But just by sitting with you, checking on you, being a sounding board or a cheerleader, they can make an enormous difference.

This might seem like it shouldn't be necessary. But there are some very good reasons why it is helpful. First of all, remember that one of the characteristics of right-brained thinkers is to be more sensitive than other people. This includes not only sensitivities to the environment, but also (and maybe even especially) sensitivities to other people. This makes using other people to help you potentially a very powerful tool.

Since you, like Kelly, were in school, you've always been sensitive to the people around you. When you're a student, teachers are around you a lot, and they influence you tremendously. Students who learn this about themselves often figure out how to use this to their advantage when they go on to college. They might sign up for more classes than they plan to complete, and go to the first week of all of their classes. They can tell immediately which teachers will hold their attention, as well as their respect. They take the classes taught by those teachers, and drop the rest, because they have learned that it is useless to try to work for someone with whom they do not feel a positive connection.

As a right-brained thinker, you are more likely to absorb the energy from people around you. You read body language and facial expressions more than left-brained people tend to do. Other subliminal messages also impact you instantly, and you are left with an emotional reading that often is difficult to shake. When the feelings you pick up are negative, your own feelings follow, and you often end up feeling depressed, confused, or hurt. Those emotions can interfere with any activity at all.

But when positive feelings come at you from other people, you absorb those as well, gaining emotional fuel and energy. This is not an emotional loan, it's a gift! So, if you have positive people around you, or people who feel positively about you and about what you need to do, you will gain confidence, energy, and enthusiasm just from being around them.

If you have some difficult organizational work to do, such as filing papers, paying bills, sorting through items, or making some tough decisions, arrange to have a friend or family member just be with you while you do it. It should be someone from whom you tend to absorb positive energy. It is not necessary for the person to actually help you at all, but only for that person to be present with you.

This helps for a number of reasons. Many people who are very right brained tend to get lost in their own thoughts, living "in their heads." This is most common in AD/HD people who tend to be spacey and inattentive, rather than hyperactive. If this is you, then having someone with you helps keep you grounded in present reality. You may start to get lost in your own dream world. But the presence of another person will keep you from getting quite so off track.

Most AD/HD right-brained people have had more than their share of difficulties and frustrations with organizational tasks, and have lost confidence in their abilities. Your self-doubt will sap your energy and take you off track. But if you have someone with you, by bouncing your concerns off a neutral person, you can interrupt your natural self-doubt and second guessing. This is more difficult to do by yourself, because your natural state is to doubt yourself.

Finally, you are used to disappointing yourself. You stop in the middle of a project, get discouraged, or get off track. You're familiar with the pattern, and with the self-recrimination that follows. Disappointing yourself is par for the course. But disappointing someone else is very different. In fact, you're probably quite bothered by how you disappoint other people, and, though you don't always succeed, you try very hard not to. You won't want to disappoint your friend. Having that person with you during difficult organizational tasks gives you an extra reason not to quit.

Part II

The Program

5

Week 1 Setting the Stage

We are what we repeatedly do. Excellence then, is
not an act, but a habit.
Aristotle

It takes thirty days to create a new habit . . .

Creating Something New

The AD/HD brain likes to play. It thrives on positive rewards
and positive feedback. So have some fun with your new project.

You will need only a few things:

■ A little bit of space.
■ A little bit of time.
■ A little bit of help.

Fueling Yourself

This program is a strength-training program for the brain. This turns out to have clear similarities to strength training for the body. In order to build strength, you will need to have the necessary building blocks. The short version of this is that you need to take care of your body in order to strengthen your mind. Chapter 3 summarizes what we recommend that you do in order to have the best chance of making this program work for you.

Many people with AD/HD "live in their heads." If you are one of these people, you find that life can get so exciting, the search for stimulation so compelling that the ordinary, boring tasks of life, like eating and sleeping, take a back seat. If you have more of the inattentive type of AD/HD, then preparing nutritious meals and keeping track of a good sleep schedule are just too boring to get much of your focus. For the next four weeks, we suggest that you take a little better care of yourself.

But the mind and body are not separate. They work together. Taking care of your body is going to make your mental training easier. Please don't misunderstand us. We are not suggesting a radical body makeover to go along with this program. We are only recommending basic attention to general good nutrition with plenty of protein, adequate sleep, and a little light exercise. These simple things make an enormous difference in mental stamina.

Making Space

Just as many people with AD/HD may neglect the impact of the physical self on the mental self, many ignore the effect of the physical space on the mental self. Because you may find it difficult to keep your physical space organized, you may have learned to live with environmental chaos. The fact that you have learned to live with it does not negate the possibility that the chaos around you results in internal chaos.

A large number of people with AD/HD are extremely sensitive to many aspects of the environment around them, including their physical space. If this is you, you might appear to be compulsively neat, because you spend so much time ordering your space. You might never get to the important tasks in your life because you spend so much time fixing up your physical space.

A healthy balance lies somewhere in between. It will distract you if you are looking at a disordered physical space. And it will keep you from moving forward if your physical space is all that you can think about. What we will be asking you to do is simply focus on a space that is small enough for you to keep orderly, and large enough to give you a visually peaceful place.

Day 1

This day is for creating a positive context in which to learn this program. You will be clearing your mind and your space for something new. And you will be setting up the positive feedback you need to keep going. It will probably be the most time-intensive day of the program. And we don't want you to spend more than *sixty to ninety minutes*.

Do not work to the point of fatigue.

You should finish each activity of this program feeling that you could do more.

Activity

With your eyes closed, picture a place in your home that you can make into a space that is uncluttered, calm, quiet, and free of distractions.

Before you close your eyes, remember that THIS CANNOT BE YOUR ENTIRE HOUSE. Even if your entire house is cluttered, chaotic, noisy, and full of distractions, you only need ONE space where this can be different. It might be a chair in a corner, a particular chair or corner that you like. You may be fortunate enough to have a room of your own. If that room is cluttered, choose one part of it that you will clear today. The place you choose may be outside, perhaps on a porch. The place might not yet exist, and you may need to create it.

As you picture this place, see yourself doing what is necessary to create your space. If it means throwing some things away, picture yourself gathering the trash, tying up the bag, and putting the bag in the trash can. Picture yourself moving a few stacks of papers aside WITHOUT READING ANYTHING. Imagine the space, the lighting, the sound, the feeling.

Now, close your eyes and take a deep breath. Keep your eyes closed while you see a vivid picture of today's activity. Remember what we have said about creating a vivid image. The more detailed and clear, the more power it will have. This power is the force that allows you to take your image and turn it into reality.

With that picture in mind, create your space. To help maintain your focus:

- Spend no more than a total of one hour.

- Divide that hour into twenty-minute segments.

- Use a timer to stop yourself in order to take a break. (Take a short walk, have a cup of tea, or just do something else entirely.)

Activity

Some time during the day, think about a way to reward yourself for completing your first week. It is vital that you plan this now, because it is crucial that you reward yourself immediately when you have finished your work and have earned your reward. The significance of this activity is that you are getting ready now for the end of week 1. If you need to, review the "Creating Rewards" section on page 80.

This particular activity involves not only knowing what you want for a reward, but also making it possible for you to obtain that reward immediately upon completing your first week of this program. So, for example, if you want a night out without the kids, find the sitter now. If you want to see a movie, decide on the one you will see now. If you want to buy something for yourself, like a new CD, a pair of shoes, Godiva chocolates, or a good bottle of wine, make sure that you have set aside the time at the end of the week to go right out and get your reward.

That's it. You've finished day one, the most difficult day of the program!

Day 2

Go to your special space. You created it as a setting for calm and focus. It's time to start using it.

Today, you will begin simple visualization exercises. It is the first day of a systematic training program to get you into the habit of using your visual brain. Like any training program, it builds skills in sequence. You might be tempted to jump ahead, to get to the "good part." We don't recommend that, because the sequence of the program is designed for building success. Early failure can be discouraging. If you try a flying sidekick in your first week of martial arts training, there's a good chance you'll suffer an injury that will sideline you for a while. However, this program is a guide for you to use as you see fit.

Activity

Think about what you need to do today. Then, pick three things that you can do in sequential order. It makes no difference what three things you pick, as long as you can do them in order. After you have the image in mind, you will then actually complete the sequence.

With your eyes closed, you will visualize yourself doing these things. Use vivid, specific detail as you visualize.

For example, let's say that one of the tasks is to return a video that you have rented. See yourself checking the case to make sure that the correct video is actually in it. See the case itself, with the title of the movie, and the picture that might be on the cover. See yourself getting to the store, whether it's by walking or driving, and picture the route along the way.

If the next thing you need to do is to arrange dinner with a friend, see yourself dialing the phone, see your calendar with you as you call, and see yourself writing down the time and the name of the restaurant.

The last thing on your list of three things might be to put in a load of laundry. Picture yourself in the laundry room or the Laundromat. See the sorted clothes, your reading material if you're at the Laundromat, the detergent, any coins you need in your pocket, or dollar bills for the coin machine. Resist the urge to skip any one of the steps or to fly through the images. Each step is integral to the whole.

As you can see, each of the tasks is pictured in detail. The details are very important, because they create a more vivid image, one that will stay in your mind, and one that has in it all of the information that you need in order to succeed.

And as you create your image for the day, make sure that you see the tasks in order. Creating that order is part of your task for today, so don't let anything else intervene in your visual image.

At the beginning it may take some time to get all the details into your image, just as each paragraph above takes some time to read. But as you hone your visualization skill, the process of creating a vivid image will become more efficient. You will need to invest some amount of time in creating these images. But the few minutes you spend can save hours later on. If you have any doubt about this, just remember the last time you came home from the supermarket with everything except the one thing you really needed.

Once you have your image clearly in mind, open your eyes. Refer to your image and check to see that it is clear. Closing your eyes again, or gazing upward without moving your head, are ways to help to see your image clearly.

Now, go ahead and execute the sequence. Check back with your image as often as you need to during the day.

How did you do? If you completed the sequence in order, that's great. If not, think about what interfered. Were your images vivid? Had you put them in a realistic order? Did you refer to the image during the day? Did you let yourself get distracted by other things?

Over the next four weeks, you'll be practicing this sort of thing, and you'll be able to improve your success rate. Each day you practice this exercise, you will make progress.

Day 3

Activity

Put something that pleases you in your space. It can be anything at all with a positive association for you. Perhaps it is a photograph. You might have a favorite piece of art that you can move to your space. A small vase with a single fresh flower could do something special for you. Maybe it's your Frisbee, or a picture of the new snowboard you're saving for.

You are not starting a collection. Now that you have just

un-cluttered your space, it is not time to fill it up again. You simply are putting something that brings you positive feelings into your space.

Activity

Continue to keep your space clear. You can be messy in every other area of your life, but not here. This makes your steps toward organization actually doable.

Activity

Visualize another three-step sequence. Remember to close your eyes and make a vivid mental image of yourself carrying out those actions.

If one of the things that you plan to do that day is go to a meeting, start your visualization at the beginning of that task. See yourself getting dressed for the meeting, and see what you are wearing. Visualize yourself as you gather the materials you will need for the meeting. See yourself putting them in your briefcase or folder. See yourself driving to the meeting, parking the car, and arriving at the meeting room, calm and prepared. See the meeting room, the other people who will be at the meeting, and the clock, showing that you have arrived a few minutes early.

Perhaps one of the things you need to do is to shop for dinner. Picture the meal you will prepare, and the specific items you need to purchase that day. See yourself walking into the butcher shop, and asking for the number of pounds of meat that you need. See yourself at the spice aisle in the supermarket, adding the two herbs that you need to your shopping cart. See yourself double-checking your list before you leave to make sure that you have everything you need.

Once you have your image clearly in mind, execute the sequence.

Day 4

Activity

Spend some more time clearing your space, if necessary. Thirty minutes is the most time that you should spend. In order to make this most productive, visualize yourself doing the task before you begin.

You are clearing out a physical space in order to create mental space. That is all that is necessary. At the end of the month, when you have finished the program, you can begin sorting through decades of papers. You just can't do it today.

Activity

Visualize a four-step sequence and carry it out.

If you've been having trouble with the three-step sequences, try simplifying the tasks. You can back way up and make the tasks much smaller. You might decide that the tasks are to (1) brush your teeth, (2) take a shower, (3) get dressed, (4) eat breakfast. You will be building the same skills as you would with more complex tasks, as long as you visualize clearly what you are going to do and stick to the sequence.

Today, for the first time, you will need someone to help you. You will need the person only for a short time. And what you will need them to do will be simple. But pick someone who will be able to be patient and who can treat this very simple activity with respect.

Activity

Jeffrey calls this the "library exercise" because he often works with students in a library, and it is easy for him to use a library as a setting. Jeffrey has his student close his or her eyes, and then he describes a detailed sequence of activities as if the student were carrying them out. Then the student repeats back what he or she can remember of what was heard.

So, it might go something like this: "You get up from your chair and walk over to the fiction stacks. You see a book with a green cover. As you get closer, you see written on the book jacket the title, *Treasure Island*. You take the book off the shelf and walk back toward your seat. You pass a water fountain and take a long drink. The water is very cold. You continue to your seat, and pass another bookshelf. You see a red book with black lettering. The title is *The Wizard of Oz*. That's the one you really want. You take it off the shelf. The cover is very smooth. You walk back to where you got the first book and put it back where you found it. You take the red book back to the seat with you. As you sit down, you look out of the window and you notice that clouds are forming. You wonder if you are going to get wet on your way home." Then it's the student's turn to repeat back as much as he or she can remember.

Did you notice the details in Jeffrey's description? He mentions a red book, black lettering, and cold water. These details make the image more memorable. Have your helper read this section so that they understand the importance of specific details.

When you do this exercise yourself, sit quietly with your eyes closed while your helper describes a sequence to you. The helper may want to use your actual location, for ease and simplicity. But it doesn't matter at all what the content is, as long as it describes you as the person acting out the sequence, and uses vivid detail. As your helper talks, you visualize yourself doing what he or she describes.

Open your eyes and repeat back as much of the sequence as you can. See how good your memory is? It's amazing what people who think that they have terrible memories are able to remember once they visualize.

You only have to do this exercise once. But, if you enjoy this and have a willing partner, do this for practice from time to time.

Day 6

Today you will start visualizing number sequences.

Don't panic because you're "no good at math." First of all, you may be much better than you think at math but not good at doing what was asked of you at school. But, more important, this isn't even math. It's just numbers.

Activity

Simply write three single-digit numbers down on a piece of paper. Look at them, and spend as much time as you need to make sure that you have them clearly in mind. Close your eyes to check to see if you have visualized them correctly. If you don't have them visualized correctly, look at them again until you do.

Open your eyes and recall the numbers, both forwards and backwards.

After you can do this correctly with three numbers, then do it with four, then five. Learn them forwards and backwards. If you are having trouble, then try using different colors as you write the numbers. This will make them easier to picture.

Don't go any further than a five-number sequence.

Activity

Visualize a four-step sequence and carry it out.

Activity

Continue to keep your space clear.

Day 7

Today, you will begin a process that is designed to slow down your thinking, to visualize what you will do, and then act. Slowing down and visualizing is the cornerstone of harnessing your strength, and this is another arena in which to practice and use this skill. We call this process "dialogue on paper."

Activity

Imagine a simple dialogue between two people, any two people. What is said is not important. How you write the dialogue is important.

As you imagine each line of the dialogue, picture the words. After you can see the words, clearly, in your mind, write them down. (This exercise helps with spelling, but that is only a bonus.)

If you want to write Shakespeare, feel free to do so, if you can visualize the words. But it's just as useful to do something much more basic, like this:

"What do you want to have for dinner?"
"I don't know. What do you want?"
"I'm in the mood for seafood."
"Then let's go out for dinner."

Do this exercise for about ten minutes.

We hope you will notice that it is easier to be clear and accurate in what you say and what you write down when you slow down and make a clear picture in your mind before you act. One of the problems that people with AD/HD have with organization is that they act impulsively and, therefore, inaccurately. Although the default position for AD/HD is "go," a great deal can be gained from learning to stop.

Activity

Continue number sequences, beginning where it was last challenging, and going up as far as eight numbers if you can, and if you want to. Spend only five or ten minutes doing this.

Activity

Visualize a four-step action sequence and complete it.

Reward for Week 1

You did it! You finished the first week.

It's time for your reward. Get it NOW. You finished the work now. And you need to have the reward NOW.

It is vital that you reward yourself immediately after doing something demanding. You have plenty of painful feelings associated with difficult tasks. Whenever you have the chance, replace those negative associations with positive ones.

Enjoy!

6

Week 2 A Picture Is Worth a Thousand
Sticky Notes

A Trail of Memos

Artists are entitled to be eccentric, reasoned Tim. But as he sat at his easel, looking around his studio at the end of a long burst of creativity, he feared that he had crossed over the line and was now officially in "bizarre" territory. Multicolored sticky notes covered almost every horizontal and vertical surface other than his canvases. They even created a path to the door.

Tim unfolded himself from his chair and stretched his lean, lanky body. Brilliant at the fine detail and subtle colorings of his paintings, he was clumsy and gangly. This gave him a childlike look that belied his serious inner nature, and fueled his family's belief that he was "immature." Tim explored the paper trail from his easel to the door. Since he had never used them, they were not reminders now, but were history, a sort of a loose-leaf diary.

A bright yellow note said, "Remember to call Mom—birthday."

He lifted a pile of rags that had buried the clock. It was midnight; he'd missed his mom's birthday, again. "Feed the cat," instructed an electric blue note. No wonder his pet had been yowling and meowing so annoyingly for the last few hours. "Order white paint," he'd commanded himself on a bright pink square. He thought that one would have mattered enough to remember. "Clean kitchen," reminded another colorful note. He walked to his bedroom through the kitchen without switching on the overhead light.

What good was this going to do? These notes were not reminders of anything, if Tim never looked at them. They had become, in his world, the equivalent of wallpaper.

Tim might have passed into the realm of the bizarre in his sincere and purposeful effort to keep himself organized. But he was sincerely trying one more strategy to keep himself on track. In writing color-coded notes to himself, and in leaving them in easy and obvious places, he was following the advice of experts. This advice, based on some sound ideas, misses the crucial distinction between verbal, left-brained thinkers and visual, right-brained thinkers.

It's Not What You See on Your Desk, It's What You See in Your Mind

The key issue for visual thinkers is how they store information, not how they take it in. All of the external strategies in the world have limited value because they ignore the necessity of the visual person activating a vivid mental image.

For example, out of sight is truly out of mind for many people with AD/HD. An ordinary filing system is unlikely to work for these people, because if an item is placed in a file for practical purposes it ceases to exist. Files may work as archives, but they do not work as a part of an organizational system.

Visual thinkers tend to be "pilers" rather than "filers" because they need to see things, to be reminded of their importance by their presence. "Don't touch my piles!" they scream, if you try to straighten up, claiming they know where everything is. Sometimes, incredibly, they can go right to what they need. Sometimes, however, they spend hours looking for that all-important statement from the IRS.

So strategies for visual thinkers are based on their visual style. Organizing experts rightly try to create systems that use visual cues. They suggest color coding, using things like colored markers, sticky notes, files, and labels. They may recommend that files be out and visible, rather than in drawers. These are tools to capture the attention of the visual, AD/HD thinker. They make sense. But they only deal with what is on your desk, or what is in your literal visual field.

But the essence of visual thinking is not what you *see*. It is what you visualize *in your mind*. The picture in your mind is how a memory is encoded or made permanent. Visual thinkers need their memories to be visual images.

What visual people see in the real world is never as vivid as what they see in their minds. Focusing on the concrete world is an iffy proposition. The colored sticky notes might seem like clutter or distractions. Or they may be easy to ignore. They may be such annoyances that an AD/HD person is motivated to ignore them.

Since they know they have bad memories, AD/HD people learn to depend on external props, like PDAs and day planners. The hazard in this method is that many people get somewhat lazy when they write things down, and they don't do the important work of activating their memories. But if the PDA fails or they leave their day planner behind (somewhere that they may not be able to remember), then they are at a complete loss.

People with a visual thinking style are holistic thinkers. They do not necessarily start at the beginning of a project. They might start with the end point and work their way back. They need to see the whole in order to keep track of its parts. But ordinary organizational strategies are linear in their structure. Asking visual people to go step by step is a low-percentage endeavor unless each of these steps involves a vivid image.

People with AD/HD think rapidly. The methodical, step-by-step methods of linear organizational strategies are so tedious and difficult that they are almost impossible for many rapid thinkers, and truly impossible for some. They may try them, but get frustrated quickly.

Visual, right-brained people, then, have difficulty using ordinary methods of organization because those methods do not truly utilize their strengths (extraordinary ability to visualize) and still require that they use their areas of weakness (linear, verbal, left-brain thinking).

We think you see why we are working with you on your visual strengths. In week two you will continue to strengthen your skills, and you will begin to use them more practically.

Stop Is Better than Go

The default position for people with AD/HD is "go." In fact, many people with AD/HD have such a high energy level, and enter such a state of hyperfocus, that they lose track of everything else going on around them. They often do not stop even to eat or sleep. They are so susceptible to distraction that when they are focused, they do not want any interruptions to that state.

Hopefully, we all have some experience with being so engrossed in something that time does not matter, and we are in that state of "flow." It is an exhilarating experience. It is not, however, a way to live daily life. Without the basics of proper rest and diet, the AD/HD brain will not be particularly effective.

And yet the energy that AD/HD people have, the enthusiasm, determination, or even stubbornness to push through, leads them to push forward when things get difficult. If this is you, you probably have found that the less productive you are, the harder you push. This is a vicious cycle, because the harder you push, the more likely you are to be impulsive or inaccurate. The more your efforts fail, the harder you push. You can see that something needs to be done, and the best way to get something done is to keep going, no matter how scattered, distractible, or ineffective you are. The one thing you don't usually think to do is to stop. Stop, to you, means failure.

So AD/HD people have to program in a nondefault position. Stopping is not automatic. Yet that is the most effective organizing tool you have. When you stop, you have the opportunity to tune in to your visual brain, the source of your strength. When you are on the go, you are engaged in the external world. That engagement with the external world prevents you from focusing on your internal world.

In this second week of the program, we want you to remember that you do have to stop in order to practice your visual skills. But, don't worry, you don't have to stop for long! And the more you practice, the better you will get. One of the rewards of this program is that you will have more of your own time!

Day 8

The activities get a little more intense or difficult as the four weeks progress. The rewards ought to be a little more intense as well. You will need to pick rewards for the ends of each of the next three weeks. And you need to think of some midweek, smaller rewards, as well.

Activity

Spend a total of thirty minutes today, but no more than fifteen minutes at a time, thinking of various-sized rewards for yourself. Review "Satisfying the AD/HD Brain" on page 42 if you need to refresh your memory about the importance of rewards. Don't worry about the specific suggestions we have made. These are just ideas to get you started. One person's reward can be another's poison, so think about them for yourself.

Write them down. Note their different sizes. It makes sense to categorize them according to size, because sometimes you will need a small reward, and sometimes a larger one. This list can be yours indefinitely. Rewarding yourself should become a lifelong habit.

Activity

Visualize a five-step sequence and execute it.

Day 9

Activity

Today's first activity is both simple and easy. There is no pressure whatsoever. You can take as much or as little time as you need. In fact, the more relaxed you are, the better this works.

Before you get up and get going, visualize the steps in your day. If possible, you should do this before you get out of bed. It should definitely be done before you engage in any activity. This means no feeding the cat, no getting the newspaper, no making coffee, no showering, no nothing. This is first.

Take your time. Keep your eyes closed while you visualize. Remember to include vivid aspects of your upcoming day. You might imagine the smell of the coffee if you are meeting someone for coffee. You might remember opening your briefcase at the office, picturing all of the files that you will need for the day. See yourself stopping to drop off your clothes at the cleaners (instead of driving right past), and include the smell of the dry-cleaning fluid.

In each of the steps, include a time component such as seeing the clock on the wall, an image of your appointment book, or the digital time on your computer.

Open your eyes, and check back with your images. Are they clear? Are they vivid? Are they possible? If, after picturing your goals for the day, you become aware that they are not realistic, take some time to revise your plans. Then visualize your corrected goals. Stick with this until you have a clear, vivid picture.

This is an exercise in visualization. At this point, it does not matter if you actually complete these activities. All that you need to do today is picture them.

When you become proficient at this task, it will take you only a few minutes to complete it. What you want to be doing now is making your images as vivid and specific as you can. Give this exercise as much time as you can in order to create these vivid images.

Activity

Choose a reward! You probably need to go through your day before you have time for it. But give it to yourself as soon as possible.

Day 10

You are now able to hold a sequence in mind. You have your rewards in place. You are able to practice more practical applications.

Activity

Each day this week (not to scare you, but each day from now on that you want to be productive and organized . . .) spend a few minutes before you get out of bed relaxing, with eyes closed, visualizing your day. Again, this is not a test, only practice.

Begin to use your mental image to notice if you have stayed on track during the day. Check back with your mental image from time to time. At the end of the day, think about how you did. How easy or difficult was it to keep your image in mind? Were you able to use your image to keep yourself organized? Was your image a realistic image of the day?

No matter how successful or unsuccessful you may judge yourself to be at using your visualization to keep yourself on target for your day, you worked hard at trying. Now you need to give yourself a break. This runs counter to the instincts of most people with AD/HD. The impulse, no matter what the situation, is to do something.

But you have put forth a lot of effort, and now it is time to rest. Give your brain a break. It will perform better tomorrow.

Activity

Relax.

Day 11

Activity

First thing in the morning, visualize your goals for the day. Make sure that your image is vivid and that you can retrieve it without much effort before you move forward with your day. Then use that image as you go about your day. Note how your reality matches your visualization.

Activity

Twice today, for five minutes each time, write lists of random words. Start with five words. Look at the words for as long as you need to in order to be sure that you have them clearly in mind. Visualize each list exactly as it is, picturing the words themselves. Try not to use mental strategies for remembering the words, because the purpose of the exercise is to increase your visualization skills. After you have a clear image, try to recall the words. Increase the number of words you put on your list as you increase your ability to do this exercise.

Day 12

Activity

Visualize your day. Remember to do this in a relaxed state, with your eyes closed, and to make your images vivid. At the end of the day, note how well your day matched your image of it.

Getting Your House in Order

One of the common questions in a AD/HD evaluation is, "Do you have trouble throwing things away, even if they have no practical value?" Look at an AD/HD home, and you are likely to find a lot of stuff. It takes too much mental energy to think through the steps required to decide if you need something, and, if you do, where its "home" will be. So you just leave the stuff where it is. You'll get to it, eventually. You leave it out as a visible reminder that you have to do something with it. Then, like Tim's sticky notes, it becomes the equivalent of wallpaper.

Some people have developed strategies to keep their homes neat. Often, if you open their closets, you are in danger of sustaining a head injury!

If you have been distractible for your entire life, you have little experience in initiating and completing tasks, going from start to finish. You have piles of things that you plan to get to eventually. You have tools sitting around, or a sewing basket sitting open. The dishes are almost done. The bathroom is clean, but there are no towels in it. The laundry is done and folded, but the basket of clean clothes sits at the foot of your bed, waiting to be put in drawers. Maybe there are two or three baskets. Maybe you have run out of baskets and the clothes just sit in piles.

One of the many benefits of medication treatment is that you may find that you can sustain your physical and mental energy long enough to complete tasks. But, for many people, even with the proper medication, there is no plan or structure, no technique or strategy for getting your house in order. If you're used to doing a little of this and a little of that, you may not even know that you can finish an entire room before moving on to another!

By visualizing yourself taking care of your home, you can create those structures so that when you begin tasks, part of the image is the goal of completing them.

Activity

Visualize yourself cleaning your house. Don't panic! Visualizing it is much easier than actually doing it. As usual, close your eyes and relax. Picture yourself in one room doing the required tasks. Stay in that room until you finish. Then move to an adjacent room and do the same thing. Stay in that room until you finish. Continue until you have finished a general housecleaning. This isn't major spring cleaning, so don't include reorganizing your spices or polishing the silver.

As you picture yourself completing each room, see the results of the job you have done. You may see the dining room table that you have cleared of newspapers and coffee cups now shiny and polished. The mail is neatly stacked. The kitchen sink has been scrubbed. The garbage is outside in the garbage can. Make sure you see what it looks like when it is finished.

Getting Stuck and Getting Off Track

As you visualize, you may find yourself stuck because you are trying to picture yourself doing a task for which you lack skills. Maybe you have little experience with that task. Or it could be that you aren't very good at it. Or maybe you only think that you aren't good at it because you don't know how to do it. It may be that you need to gain some knowledge. You may need some assistance with that task. If so, picture yourself doing the task with that assistant. Or picture yourself getting to the end of the task, even if you are not sure how you got there.

The experience of getting stuck is one of the triggers for getting distracted. Rather than persist in something that seems too difficult, it becomes automatic to move on to something else. When it comes to keeping your house in order, that leaves the roasting pan soaking in the sink, the ironing in a basket, the groceries not put away, the mail not read, and the bills only half paid.

What is crucial about this visualization exercise, then, is to see yourself FINISHING!

If this takes too long, if even the image of cleaning several rooms is daunting, then visualize the process in just one room. You can practice this exercise as often as is comfortable. Certainly, you should use this technique when you are actually going to clean your house. For now, the main purpose is to move your practice of visualizing from the abstract to the concrete, from theoretical to practical.

Your Reward: You have been working hard. Pick a medium-sized reward. Today's reward won't be tickets to a basketball playoff game or a Broadway show. But you might want to rent a movie and relax, or get takeout for dinner, so you don't have to do any dishes.

Day 13

Activity

Visualize your day and use that image throughout the day to stay on track. As you visualize your day, you might see the clock on the wall, and register the time. You might see what time you leave home and then what time you arrive at your destination. As you see yourself driving, note the time on the clock on the dashboard. Make sure to use all of your senses in your visualization exercises. Include the radio station you usually listen to as you drive. You might feel the fuzzy collar of your coat against your face, or imagine the taste of the delicious lunch you are going to have. The more senses you use, the more vivid your image will be, and the more likely you are to have your visualizations work for you.

Activity

Visualize a close relative. Picture the person's face, clothing, way of moving. See if you can hear the person's voice, and sense his or her attitude or mood. Picture as many specific details as you can.

Day 14

Activity

Again, visualize yourself completing your full day's activities. Remember to include driving routes, items you will need to take with you, people you will see, and tasks you plan to accomplish. Remember to note the element of time if you can.

Today, you will add something to your daily visualization of your day. After you have your image clear, write down your day's full schedule of activities. Set this aside until the end of the day. Then, when your day is over, review your notes and see how close you came to remembering your day.

Keeping Your Purpose Clear

Each exercise in this program is designed to strengthen and increase your biggest strength, your power to make mental images. Nevertheless, it is helpful for most people to have a backup in writing or on a hand-held organizer. People with less ability to visualize find it easier to visualize a simple list rather than the more vivid but complex images of their planned activities.

We have waited until you have solid experience before introducing anything written, because it is easy to rely too heavily on what you have written if you are not confident in your mental image. If that happens, then you are at risk of making the common mistake of writing something down without first making an image of it.

Then it's anyone's guess whether you will actually remember to refer to what you have written.

Reward Time!

You have made it through two weeks! You deserve a big reward. You truly have earned it. This is a pretty big reward, something that you can really savor. Maybe it will be going out to dinner at a restaurant with really good service. Or perhaps you can take the afternoon off from work and go for a bike ride or see a matinee.

You should be so much better at visualizing now that some extra steps we are going to ask you to add in Week 3 should come fairly easily. So just relax and rest your brain for the next step.

7

Week 3 It's About Time!

However difficult it may be for you, getting a handle on the concept of time is a necessary part of organization. In chapter 2, we hope we got you started thinking about time. As you continue with the program, you will continue to add time concepts gradually to your visualization exercises. The final goal is for you to be factoring time into your normal routines.

How Did It Get to Be So Late?

We all have somewhat different perceptions of time. If you ask a room full of people to raise their hands when they think that a minute has passed, there will be a wide range of responses. But many people do have a sense of the passage of time. This is not necessarily the case if you are a highly visual thinker, like Lisa.

It was like clockwork for Lisa. (No pun intended.) She would notice the time and ask her husband, Henry, "How did it get to be so late?" The first fifty or so times that Lisa asked that question, Henry answered concretely, as if she really wanted to know what had happened in their day. He would tell her that it had taken a long time to paint the hallway. Or he would say that the football game had gone into overtime. Or he would remind her that she had spent an hour talking long distance to her sister.

After a couple of years of living together, Henry realized that Lisa was paying no attention to the passage of time. He thought this was a bit immature and irresponsible of her. He created his stock answer. Lisa would ask, "How did it get to be so late?" and Henry would respond, "The same way it always does."

Without the sense of the passage of time, it is difficult to estimate how long it will take to accomplish something, and so it is difficult to create and stick to a schedule that has limits and priorities. It is also difficult to meet commitments to others who expect you to be on time if you have a hard time knowing what time it is. And it often leaves you asking, once again, when you find that the day has again raced by without accomplishing what you had hoped, "How did it get to be so late?"

It got to be so late the way it always does, outside of Lisa's awareness, and outside of your awareness. Part of this program, then, is to help you find ways to bring the experience and the concept of time into your awareness in some concrete and specific ways that you can use to stay more organized. There is some thought that the experience of time is a dopamine-dependent neurological function. Medication may help, then, with a better awareness of time. There are also ways to use your visual skills to gain a better sense of time.

Digital or Analog

How do you make an image of something that doesn't look like anything, because it has no substance to it? At some point, you might get creative about it, and come up with your own personal image of the passage of time. But a universal and practical picture of the passage of time is, simply, a clock.

In today's fast-paced, computerized, digital age, most clocks now are digital. They give us accurate time. However, as you see numbers changing, they fly by just like time itself. They don't help in visualizing time in a concrete way. Your image needs to be concrete in order to make it real.

Analog clocks, the old-fashioned kind with a face, give us a more useful image of time. You can see chunks of it as slices of a pie. This concept is so useful that a company called Time Timer supplies an assortment of timers in which a red wedge shows the amount of time with which you are working. As time elapses, the wedge shrinks. It is hard to continue to believe that you have all the time in the world as you see it disappearing. A quarter hour or a half hour each has an actual shape that you can see in your mind and that you can gradually and naturally incorporate into your visualization process. This is a more vivid and useful image than pure numbers as you work to integrate a sense of time into your visual memory.

Activity

Each day this week, visualize your day's activities. Picture an image of time with each one. See the actual clock on your kitchen wall as you finish breakfast, see the one in your car as you drive, see yourself checking your watch, as you picture these activities. At the end of the day, observe how your actual day unfolded compared to your image.

This idea of time needed for each thing is often revolutionary for people with AD/HD. It sounds weird, but people with AD/HD often live as if the things that are boring or that they don't care about don't require any real time. Out of sight, out of mind is one thing. Out of mind, out of time is even worse!

For example, it actually takes time to walk from the parking lot, into the mall, and to a specific store. When people with AD/HD plan a trip to the mall, however, they often leave out that sort of detail. So, for example, Amy may figure it will take her a half hour to purchase some new makeup.

Amy does something that is extremely common for people like her. She has the idea of one half hour in mind as the time it will take to complete her purchase. However, if it is a busy time, it might take a few minutes to find a parking space. After she parks the car, she has to rummage through her purse to find the coupon she's been carrying around that will give her a special price on the makeup. When she finds it and sees that it expired last month, she decides to get the makeup anyway, because she's already at the mall, and she needs it. She gets out of the car, locks it, and takes a few steps before she realizes that she has left her cell phone behind. She turns around and goes back to get it. (This is Ratey's "pirouette sign.")

After retrieving her cell phone, Amy continues to walk to the department store. It's about five minutes to get there from the parking lot. She knows she's got limited time, so she works hard not to linger at any of the displays as she walks through the mall.

When she gets to the makeup counter, there is one woman ahead of her. In her mind, being next in line means that at any moment it will be her turn. She has no idea, really, how long she might have to wait, and therefore never factored it into her time frame. It turns out not to be too bad. The woman ahead of her completes her purchase in ten minutes. Now it's Amy's turn. It does take her about a half an hour to choose the right shade of makeup and have it specially mixed for her.

She's been at the store long enough that she needs to go to the ladies' room before driving back home. That's down the hall a little way. Between getting there and using the facility, that's another eight minutes.

Okay, let's try adding this up. Three minutes to park the car. Two minutes to rummage through her purse. Three minutes to start off and return to the car to get the cell phone. Five minutes to get to the store. Ten minutes to wait for the customer in front of her. Eight minutes for a bathroom break. Five minutes to get back to the car. That's *thirty-one* extra minutes. It took Amy twice as long as she had thought it would to buy her makeup.

This is not an unusual example. And it is precisely these little bits of time that we want you to start seeing as you visualize your day. If you know you are out of gas, visualize yourself getting to the gas station, getting out of the car, putting your credit card in the machine, choosing the quality of gasoline, and finally pumping the gas (unless you live in New Jersey, in which case you visualize yourself waiting for the service person to pump the gas for you). Remember to put the gas cap back on. See yourself leaving the gas station and getting back on the route to where you are going. As you look at these details, you can see that they clearly do not take zero time, though they might be of zero interest to you!

Day 16

Okay, so do we have to rub it in? Or is it clear that you can't estimate how long it's going to take to do things, because you really have very little idea of how much time real things actually require? Today, you'll start finding out!

Activity

Visualize your day's activities, as usual, including visuals of time.

Activity

Pay attention to how long it actually takes to do the things you have to do. This requires that you basically take a microscopic look at your day, something you are not used to doing. You may need help from someone else to start to think about the many things you actually have to do. We mean for you to note the amount of time it takes for you to do all the little things in your day. And in order to be able to complete this activity, you may need to think of your world in a whole new way.

Instead of thinking that you have to "get up and go to work," you need to think of the specific steps you take to accomplish that goal. You will need to start with your daily visualization. Then you will include each step, especially things that you do automatically or that you don't think of as unique, individual steps. So, for example, you will want to notice how long it takes to make coffee, take a shower, shave, do your hair, get dressed after your shower, locate two of the same earring, find the things you need for work, make breakfast, eat breakfast, take vitamins or medications, brush your teeth, find your wallet and keys, walk to the subway, walk to work, drive to work, park the car, lock the car, go back to get what your forgot from the car. You get the picture. Break down your day into tiny pieces, if you have to, to make sure that you include the time required for everything.

Is that enough for one day?

Day 17

Activity

Today's activity is just like yesterday's activity with one important addition: After you complete your visualization, quickly write down your schedule for the day, including the time factor.

This written schedule is to help you evaluate your estimates. It is not a substitute for your active visual memory. As we have pointed out before, relying on external supports to the exclusion of your strong visual memory is what you most likely already do, and it does not serve you well. As part of this program, the written schedule is only to give you a way to measure your progress, not to substitute for visualization.

At the end of the day, see not only how well you were able to maintain your schedule, but also how accurately you allotted time for yourself.

Break Down and Buy a Watch

Let's revisit Henry and Lisa. Henry was starting to become resentful. Why, he wondered, could Lisa blithely go through her days, not thinking about, not being concerned about, not worrying about, not being the least bit burdened by awareness of the time? Must be nice, he thought. But he was tired of being the family timekeeper. He resigned from his position.

They were late for quite a few things before Lisa started to think for herself about the time. She wasn't completely clueless. But, since time awareness didn't come easily to her, she had relaxed and enjoyed having Henry take responsibility for it. She had a revelation which led her finally to take a step that, to left-brainers is utterly obvious, but for her was a major decision.

That's right. Lisa did not own a watch. Watches irritated her wrist. She lost them or wore them in the shower. Someone else always had one. So she gave up on having one herself. It had been so long since she had shopped for one that she was a bit overwhelmed by the choices, styles, and prices available. Only by sheer luck, because she didn't want to spend much, did she end up with what was just right for her: a plain watch with a regular clock face, large numbers, and a sweep second hand.

The distaste that people with AD/HD have for keeping track of time often has emotional factors as well as neurological ones. People with AD/HD hate to be tied down. It feels restrictive to them. They feel they don't want to cut off their options. The reality is that their difficulty in holding numerous or disparate ideas in mind at once makes it hard for them to make choices. The experience of having to choose is so burdensome that they eliminate it whenever possible.

Making lemonade out of lemons, or a virtue out of necessity, people with AD/HD see themselves as easygoing or freewheeling. They see people who keep track of time or of the need to make decisions in a timely fashion as "type A" or as "worriers" or as, God forbid, "anal." But the truth is, without planning, their lives do not progress as they would like. Opportunities pass by. There really is a difference between being "anal" and being organized. We are only helping you achieve the latter.

You may think that you don't need a watch, because you can always keep track of the time without one. You're kidding yourself. Get a watch.

Activity

Supply yourself with timepieces. This means go shopping and buy whatever you need to enable you to keep track of time.

This activity is optional in that some people will need to do it and some people will not. We hope that you will be honest about recognizing if this is an essential activity for you.

Every room in your house should have at least one easily visible, easy-to-read clock. The tiny digital clock on your computer does not count. This needs to be a real clock that you can see from across the room. As you learn to gain a better sense of time, you need it to be hard to avoid!

You will also need a wristwatch. It should be large and easy to read so that just glancing at it allows you to see what time it is.

If you decide on a wall clock, make sure that you have the supplies for hanging it. If a clock is going to require batteries, buy them now. If you're on a tight budget, bite the bullet and buy the cheapest clock you can find. The least expensive ones often turn out to be the best for this project. They are large and very plain. They have numbers, not artistic dots. They have plain hour and minute hands that clearly point to those numbers. They do the job.

Day 18

You're doing great! Today's activities will be reviews, so that you can consolidate what you are learning.

Activity

Again, visualize your day's activities, incorporating the element of time. Jot down your schedule and refer to it at the end of the day. How did you do?

Activity

Have you picked out your big reward for the end of the program? You may well feel that completing the program is, itself, a reward. We hope that you end up feeling that way, and think it is most likely that you will. But that isn't enough. When the going gets tough, you need extra help pulling yourself forward toward completing your goal.

Can you take a whole day off from work and go fishing? How about a spa day, with a massage and pedicure? Maybe you don't need, but really would like, a new pair of classy gold earrings? Perhaps, for you, a reward would be a visit to the new Museum of Modern Art, for twenty dollars, even though you remember when it was only five? Maybe it's your own personal film festival in which you see three or four movies in a row, including ones that no one you know wants to see?

Plan it now.

Day 19

Activity

Remember to make a habit of visualizing your day before you get out of bed. Include images of the amount of time it will take to do things. Briefly write down your plans. Check at the end of the day to see how you did.

Activity

Pick an activity from week one or two. Note the progress you have made.

Day 20

Activity

Visualize your day's activities, first thing in the morning. Remember to include time in your visualization. Jot down your plan. At the end of the day, compare what you planned to what you actually did.

Gaining Perspective

One of the tasks of the brain's right hemisphere is to orient you in space. You use it when you read maps, play ball sports, do gymnastics, martial arts, dance, and so forth. This skill is useful in reading blueprints, painting, drawing, computer graphics, and computer games, among many other activities.

This spatial ability is usually quite active in people with AD/HD. Many have found work and other interests that capitalize on this ability. They can see things from many different perspectives, and so are good problem solvers. Or they can visualize the cabling in an entire building or an entire auto engine in their mind's eye, giving them excellent skills when working in those arenas.

However, people who can see things from many different angles often find themselves seeing several of those different perspectives simultaneously or in such rapid succession that the picture becomes a blur. These images seem to move out of a person's control.

This is one of the areas in which it is easy to see how medications can be helpful, because it gives the person the ability to stop the image, even freeze-frame it, long enough to do something with it rather than watching it whiz by. Working with those images and practicing the ability to focus on them is important, with or without medication.

The ability to see things from different perspectives is essential for creativity. It is also vital for empathy with others. These are strengths typical of the right-brained person with AD/HD. However, when the ability to use perspective is not channeled, it can lead to the opposite of creativity or empathy. Not being able to organize different perspectives, and find a grounded center in the middle of all of those thoughts, can lead to confusion.

This clearly interferes with creativity and productivity, because the confusion doesn't lead to creative outcome or solutions, but only to chaos. And it interferes with empathy because it is difficult to know, literally, whose feelings are whose when so many perspectives swim around. The apparent thoughtlessness or carelessness of people with AD/HD is often not intentional, but rather due to disorganization. Confusion about interpersonal conflicts is one of the distractions that people with AD/HD experience, a distraction that drains emotional energy as well as productivity.

Most people don't think about using spatial ability to plan out and program activities. Those without spatial ability are more likely to benefit from linear methods, including typical lists and schedule planners. But if you are reading this book, working with your spatial ability will be one more way to help maximize your strength.

Activity

Imagine yourself as someone else in your daily life, whether it is your boss, boyfriend, girlfriend, spouse, sibling, or coworker. Put yourself in that person's shoes. How do you look to them? Look from their eyes. How do they see others? What is it like to be that person? What are their loves and what are their fears?

By "being" someone else, you are practicing your ability to view things in perspective. This ability requires your holding one point of view at a time. This is a necessary step in increasing your ability to stay organized. In order to set priorities, make decisions, and move forward, you must first be clear where you stand. If you keep spinning from one idea to another, from one point of view to another, you will be exhausted and you will not have made any progress.

Day 21

Activity

Visualize your day's activities. You know the drill.

Activity

Practice visualizing single words in a book or magazine. Look at a word until you have a clear image of it. Then, close your eyes and remember the word clearly. How is it spelled? What is the fourth letter? How many syllables does it have? Can you spell it backwards?

Stopping in Order to Start

Jack loved his Saturday projects. They didn't seem like work to him. Work was sitting at a desk, filling out paperwork. Whew, was that ever work! But Jack's projects at home were recreation. He was using his hands, building, creating, sweating. It was all fun for him, and filled him with creative energy.

As he finished repairing a huge old gilt mirror that he had scavenged from a garage sale, he realized that he would need extra-strong hooks and wire to hang it. Eager to see the mirror on the wall, he grabbed his keys and wallet and ran off to the hardware supermarket to get what he needed. He'd only be gone for a minute, so he didn't bother to tell Ann he was going.

He was so single-minded, it never occurred to him to think if he might need anything else. He made two more trips to the same store that same day, once for washers to repair a dripping faucet in the laundry room, and once for a toggle switch for his desk lamp.

One of the common characteristics of sensitive, right-brained people with AD/HD is that they are quick to react. Often they are impulsive. When you are aware that something needs to be done, you may find that you either do nothing, or act quickly and automatically. That quick reactivity may feel like efficiency. But, when done without thinking, it often results in a plan as inefficient as Jack's.

Although we know that it is likely to be counterintuitive to you, by visualizing you are taking important steps in actually getting work done. By taking a very few minutes, maybe only seconds, to visualize before you act, you save huge amounts of real time (not to mention gasoline!). You might save weeks, months, or even years of time spent inefficiently organized.

By going back and doing an exercise you have already done, you have practiced slowing down. Your impulse is to look for something new. You deserve credit for having the strength to do something old. You deserve a reward.

Activity

Pick a small reward for slowing down.

Focus

The active, visual right-brained person is often brimming with ideas. In order to be organized, however, it is necessary to take these ideas one at a time. Even if the thinking process is not linear, it still is necessary to have some focus. Otherwise, the multitude of ideas tumbling over each other becomes overwhelming. All of this leads to cognitive overload, and the feeling that there's too much to do; anxiety and panic take over, and nothing gets done.

Singling out one particular word and focusing on that one word helps in dealing with overload. Although it often seems that you have to focus on everything at once, it helps to build your ability to focus on only one thing at a time.

Focus is another area in which the need for medication often becomes apparent. Difficulty inhibiting thoughts that you don't want is one of the common characteristics of AD/HD. There are some circumstances in which no amount of "mind over matter" can change the way your thoughts bounce around. The exercises in this program are designed to be simple and to progress in a stepwise fashion. If you find that no amount of practice or effort seems to allow you to narrow down your focus, you might want to consider adjusting or adding medication.

The End of Week 3

Wow! Almost done! Don't forget to reward yourself.

It is typical for people with AD/HD to accept lots of blame for things they do wrong, and to fail to notice what they do right. You have to practice feeling good about what you do well. Getting this far deserves recognition, don't you think? Have fun. See you tomorrow.

8

Week 4 Bringing It All Together

Are You Making Progress?

Toni, with her flowing blond hair and easy laugh, found that she charmed people easily. Her lively conversation and broad range of interests made people want to spend time with her. So she had a busy social life, many boyfriends, and tried lots of things.

But the same liveliness that attracted so many to her and that made her so interesting was part of a long-standing and relentless distractibility. One experience led her to look for another, and one relationship led her to look for another. Nothing in her life, therefore, was continuous. She had lots of great ideas, but few led to fruition. And she had made lots of friends, but couldn't follow through enough to sustain relationships.

There was no question that she meant well and tried to do her best. She was so impaired by her impulsivity and distractibility as well as by her creativity that she had no ability to stop, evaluate, plan, or sequence her activities. Unlike many people with AD/HD, she had not tried a lot of different systems for trying to organize herself. In fact, she hadn't tried any!

For her, treatment to slow down her thinking, to allow her to think before acting, to allow her to imagine herself as the making of her own destiny would be necessary before she could even make use of this program. Energetic and creative people often find it very difficult to accept that medication is a necessary or appropriate step for them to take. Surely they can find a way to make life work without all the negative things that go along with taking medications.

If you have been working this program and find that you are unable to get clear, vivid, accurate, images of the activities of your day, or of the exercises requiring you to visualize numbers and letters, then it's important to do a little troubleshooting. There are a number of possibilities to explain your difficulties.

You might have difficulties that are similar to Toni's in that despite your visual style, your AD/HD symptoms of distractibility and impulsivity are great enough so that you cannot slow down your mind. If you cannot slow your mind down for the short time it takes to create and focus on an image, then you cannot strengthen your visual skills. If this is the case, you should seriously consider getting a thorough evaluation for AD/HD and, as a part of that process, seeing what medication can do for you. As we have said in chapter 3, medication can be an important part of gaining the control you need of your visual skills. You may have done all you can and tried hard enough without medication, and it may be time to make use of the important tool that medication can be.

It is also possible that you might not be a visual enough learner. In other words, you might be too left brained for the visualizations to come easily to you. This program works best for those whose visual learning style is a clear strength. If you are completely left brained, this program will not help you. But if you are a person with AD/HD, there is a very high probability that you are largely a visual learner. This is all on a continuum, however. So, if you are making some progress, but find the visualizations difficult, you might be a bit farther "left" on the continuum than those for whom visualizations come easily. Give yourself a little more time with each visualization, be easy on yourself, and see if you can at least use the visualizations to add to other organizational tools that you already find useful.

Hopefully, though, you are noticing that you have a better sense of confidence in yourself as you go about your day. The strength of your memory should be clearer to you, and your clear images should help you feel calmer as you feel more and more sure that you know what you are doing!

Using this skill is a lifelong activity. But there is one more week of the specific skill-building program.

The Final Push

Before you get started with the activities of the last week, make sure that you have the basics in place.

1. Get regular sleep. Or, at least, improve your sleeping habits. For many of you, this is a catch-22. If you were better organized, you would be getting more sleep! We understand. We also know that research continues to demonstrate that better sleep quality leads to better mood, memory, focus, concentration, and effectiveness. There is no doubt about this.

2. Eat a healthy diet with plenty of lean protein and vegeta-

bles. DON'T SKIP MEALS! In fact, eating more frequent, smaller meals, each including protein, will keep your physical and mental energy even.

3. Have a space for yourself that is peaceful and uncluttered. If you give this space a small amount of care every few days, you should be able to keep it reasonably clear.

4. Make absolutely sure that you have a reward in place for the end of this week. If you don't have your reward set, arranged, financed, whatever, stop now and do what you have to do. As you push yourself to do what you otherwise would not do, keep in mind that you will get to do something great, or you will get to have something great. And it will be yours very, very soon!

Goals for the Final Week

Three things are important for this last week.

1. You will continue your daily habit of visualization.
2. You will review past exercises to make sure that you have a good grasp of the basic principles of this program, and to show to yourself how much you have improved.
3. You will integrate your new habits into more areas of your daily life.

Process, Not Product

At the end of this program, you should have a beginning set of skills that you can develop for the rest of your life. These skills will build over time. Every day that you practice, you accomplish something. It is this *process* that is important, not the *product* that results from your efforts. We know that, as a person with AD/HD, you are very good at keeping track of your faults and errors, and pretty poor at tracking and scoring your successes. In this program, every day that you work at this program counts as a success. As you make it a habit to use your right-brain strengths, your skill at visualization and your creativity in how to use this skill will continue to develop. You will create your individualized version of what you have been learning.

Your ability to imagine what "perfect" looks like makes you a harsh judge of yourself and your abilities. Do not expect perfection. Ever. Just remember that these techniques will work for you in the long term, and, probably in the short term, because they are harmonious with the way you think. They are also a constant reminder that you are not a broken left brainer, but a competent person with AD/HD, solving your organizational challenges by using your powerful, innate strengths.

Day 22

Activity

Continue your daily planning, as before. However, this week, you will add a regular evening activity to your morning planning routine.

First thing in the morning, visualize your day, as you

have been doing. Then write out your day's activities, including the time each activity will take. Visualize yourself doing them as you write them down.

In the evening, review what you have written, and how well you did. Then, close your eyes and relax. Think of tomorrow. You don't need to be concerned about visualizing accurately and specifically as you do in the morning. Rather, glance over your day in your mind's eye.

Thinking about tomorrow may stimulate you to take care of some things you might otherwise have forgotten. By all means, take action, if it's indicated. But the idea of this exercise isn't to send you scrambling around your home, making sure everything you might need is ready for the next day. Rather, it is to get you comfortable and familiar with looking into the future and seeing your day in sequence. The more you do this, the more you will be likely to find yourself better prepared ahead of time instead of scrambling at the last minute.

Day 23

Activity

Preview your day's activities, visualizing, including the element of time. Write down your schedule.

Each day for the rest of this week, you will also revisit

earlier exercises. You will see how much progress you have made. You will also notice your strengths and weaknesses and be able to troubleshoot.

For example, are you moving too quickly through your number sequences, because you've always been good at math? Do you resist focusing on individual words because you think you aren't good at spelling? Are you too restless to settle down to do a short visualization exercise?

Have you refused to accept that most things take longer than you expect, and, because of that, found that your days are still unrealistically cramped? Have you not managed to buy a watch?

Activity

Visualize a three-step sequence and carry it out. Do it again. Notice how much easier this is for you than when you first started.

See if you can do the visualization a little bit faster. Focus on the details.

Visualize a four-step sequence and carry it out. Is it any harder that the three-step one?

Activity

Remember to briefly imagine tomorrow's day at the end of the day.

Unintended Consequences

Sometimes, increased confidence and skill leads you to take on more because you can. It is very common for people with AD/HD who have improved their abilities to get very excited about what they can do. They take on more and more, and sometimes find themselves back where they started, because now their new skills are not enough to manage the new level of stress. They may be just as symptomatic as before they started treatment. They wonder why treatment isn't working. But the truth is that treatment *is* working. They have, however, assumed that they can push themselves as hard as they want. This is part of the enthusiasm and zest for life that is also a positive part of AD/HD. You just have to watch out for it as you make progress. You don't want to end up like Dan.

Dan won the top sales award at least once every three quarters, sometimes more often. He had such enthusiasm for what he was doing that he made people feel that they were lucky that he had come along, or they might have gone their whole lives without his product. This excitement made up for a few not-so-minor deficits.

Despite the efforts of every woman in his life to help him, he had never even begun to master personal grooming, and he certainly did not dress for success. Though he managed to shave everyday, he usually missed a few spots. He laundered regularly, meaning once a month whether he needed to or not. His rumpled shirts did not stay tucked into his pants, and his pants never fit quite right.

Every salesman, to some extent, lives out of his car. In Dan's case, however, it was more like living out of a dumpster. The front seat was reserved for work-related items. The back seat was piled high with sports equipment, fast food wrappers, newspapers, coffee cups, and who knows what else.

By the end of each day, Dan was so fired up on nervous energy that he invariably forgot some important piece of paperwork.

In fact, it was the paperwork that kept Dan from winning more awards than he did. Dan didn't exactly put off paperwork, though he hated it as much as anybody. He just raced through it, eager to get on to the next sales call. Invariably, he made numerous careless errors, confusing his orders, delaying invoices, and creating general chaos.

His boss didn't want to fire someone with such incredible numbers. But he found Dan to be the most difficult employee he'd ever had to manage.

For his part, Dan pushed himself so hard that he often found himself collapsing at the end of the week, and starting each week with catching up to do from the week before.

All of this chaos made Dan extremely nervous. His anxiety about getting everything done, layered on top of his high-speed style, guaranteed that his memory would fail.

Dan was doing more and was pushing himself harder. To some extent, that strategy will work. But, when the load becomes large enough, it taxes a person's cognitive capacity. At that point, pushing harder and harder produces no better outcome. But it does increase stress, and that, itself, actually reduces cognitive capacity.

Stress reduces memory. It is as simple as that. In a variety of different types of experiments, with rats or humans, stress has been shown to reduce short-term and long-term memory, attention, and concentration.

Dan is trying to work better. He is working harder. But he is not working smarter. Simply pushing himself has the unintended consequence of reducing his effectiveness. And that includes reducing his ability to stay organized. He begins to put out fires, to respond immediately to whatever someone asks him or to whatever is in front of him. In that state, he has no ability to gauge the priority of anything. He does things because they are the most urgent, but they may not be the most important.

If Dan had a picture in his mind of what he most needed to do, it would be much easier for him to keep on track. He'd be able to stay more organized. And he would know if he had planned too much to do in a single day. But, to do this, he needs to understand that his usual method of pushing himself as hard as he can has the unintended consequence of making him less productive.

Taking a Step Back

If you notice yourself becoming anxious, it may mean that you, too, are trying to do too much in a single day. The tendency to overestimate what is reasonable to accomplish and to pile on too much may already be a habit. Overestimate how much time you will need to spend on things.

Day 24

Activity

Visualize your day, including the time component. Jot down your schedule.

Activity

Visualize number sequences as you did in week 1. Today, add two or three more numbers than you were able to remember in week 1.

Activity

At the end of the day, see how your actual day compared to your planned day. Note adjustments you might make tomorrow. You may need to adjust travel time, time on the telephone, time to do shopping, and so forth.

Activity

Think about your plans for tomorrow.

Day 25

Activity

Visualize your day and jot down your plans.

Activity

At the end of the day, see how you did at executing your plans.

Activity

Visualize cleaning a room. Decide how much time you can give to this project, and see yourself doing what is possible within this time frame. Be specific and vivid. Remember that you need to see yourself doing the cleaning.

Now carry out what you saw yourself doing.

Activity

Tonight, as you think about tomorrow, take the time to visualize vividly and accurately what you plan to do.

Day 26

Activity

Visualize your day in the morning. Jot down your schedule.
In the evening, see how you did.
Visualize your next day. Make it vivid.

Activity

Pick some words out of a magazine. Look at each of them,
separately. See each word clearly. Get a vivid picture. See the
different syllables. See the letters in order. Look at the letters
of the word in your mind backwards. Do this with three or
four words. Piece of cake!

What about All the Stuff?

Jill didn't even take her coat off if there was a new decor magazine in the mail when she got home from work. Passionate about art
and design, she loved getting lost in the photos of perfect juxtapositions of old and new, bright and subtle, cozy and spare. She loved
looking at high-end homes, for inspiration. And she loved thinking
of decorating on a budget, and imagined how she could use the
ideas she found in upscale magazines for her creative, yet frugal,
projects.

Ironic, then, that there wasn't a place in Jill's home to even set down the magazine without having to balance it on a haphazard and precariously piled stack of assorted other things: an empty egg carton, yesterday's bills, a new battery for her phone, a scarf, and a recipe for an appetizer for a potluck the next day. Someday, she thought, she'd have it all cleaned up. Then she could create an environment in which she could thrive, like the ones she admired in her magazines.

How could her mental life be so different from her actual one? If she looked at her kitchen counter, would she see the chaos there? Or would the actual state of her environment, that which she could see with her eyes, hold less power over her than the internal environment, the vivid images she created in her mind?

Clearly, she preferred the looks of the homes in the magazine. But those images were a fantasy, arrived at by some mysterious path she had not yet discovered. It was a "someday" wish that she hoped would come true one day, when she had gotten her place straightened up. But Jill's visual style, the part of her that helped her visualize so clearly how she wanted her home to look, left her without the linear skills to take the steps to achieve her goal.

Organizational experts have suggested plenty of strategies for organizing the physical environment. Some are even designed by and for people with AD/HD. What they are likely to leave out is the process of actually getting to those strategies, and the difficulty in integrating those strategies into a person's actual life. Jill had read books about organization, had hired people to come help her organize her home, and understood, in an abstract way, the value of keeping her home in order. (For example, until she cleared off her kitchen counter, it wasn't apparent how she was going to prepare the appetizer she had promised to make. She might end up moving the process to the dining room, because of the lack of cleared counter space.)

Jill needs to make a mental image of each task she must complete in order to even begin. Until the reality of her cleaning up her house is vivid, like the images of her dream home, the linear process of cleaning up remains only theoretical.

Activity

Pick one small part of your home to organize. It could be the bathroom counter. It could be the stack of reading material beside the toilet. It could be the stack of mail next to the front door. It could be the recyclables.

Don't think about the whole kitchen, bathroom, or garage. In fact, you may never be very good at organizing the whole kitchen or cleaning the whole garage. You may do best, because of your ideal length of energy and concentration, always to do tasks in smaller pieces. Today's exercise is to visualize your task and to complete it, using your visualization as your guide, focus, and motivation.

Pick a task for which you already have at least adequate skills. If you've never set up files with printed labels, today isn't the day to start. But if you know how to look at magazines and create two piles, one to keep and one to toss, then that is a reasonable task.

Make sure that your image is vivid. If you are going to tie up newspapers, for example, see yourself getting the twine and scissors before you start. See yourself gathering the papers into the right-sized stacks. See yourself setting them at the curb, or the room in your apartment where you set recyclables before you take them out. See yourself putting the twine and the scissors away.

Seeing the Whole Picture

One of the critical issues in the clutter that surrounds people with AD/HD is that they do not generally include putting equipment away as part of a task. Wrapping a package ends with tying the bow. Hanging a picture ends with standing back and making sure the picture is level. Baking brownies ends with taking them out of the oven.

But the reality is that wrapping a package ends with putting the scissors and tape back in the drawer where they belong. Hanging a picture ends with putting the hammer back in the toolbox. And baking brownies ends with washing up the bowls, cups, and spoons.

When you visualize your thing-organizing tasks, you will start small, but you will see yourself completing the task. Having that image will guide you through the task, including its completion. Bit by bit, scissors by scissors, egg crate by egg crate, newspaper by newspaper, the clutter will begin to recede.

Clutter control is an ongoing project. By breaking it into small pieces that can be finished, the theoretical becomes the practical. The fantasy is still that, a fantasy. An image of perfection is not an attainable goal. But shifting directions from increasing to decreasing chaos is an attainable and a very realistic goal.

Day 27

Activity

Visualize your day. You know the drill. See how you did at the end of the day.

Activity

At the end of the day, see your day for tomorrow. Include the time component.

Activity

Pick another area of your home that is cluttered. It could be the stack next to the one you tackled yesterday, or it could be somewhere entirely different. Close your eyes and relax. Visualize tackling that area. But today, break the task down into discrete steps that you see yourself doing.

For example, let's say you decide to clean out the medicine chest. Step one would be to get a large garbage bag for items to throw away and a large box for the things you plan to keep. Step two would be to take everything out of the medicine chest. If you have a counter, you can empty it onto the counter. If you don't have a counter, then you may need to bring in a third box or a card table so that you can see your items. Step three would be to toss the things that you don't need, don't use, or that have expired. Step four would be to clean out the inside of the medicine chest. Step five would be to put the items you are going to keep back into the medicine chest. Step six would be to put the trash out, put the boxes away, and put away the folding table.

See yourself doing each step. Imagine yourself laughing as your find four packages of dental floss, each on a different shelf of the medicine chest. Marvel as you find leftover antibiotics from seven years ago. See yourself getting rid of the trash.

Whatever task you imagine, see yourself doing the individual steps, from gathering your materials to putting them away.

Well done!

Almost Done

Easier than you thought? And a bit anticlimactic? Did you think your whole house would be clean? Did you think you would never forget anything, again? We hope we haven't led you to believe you'd be perfect. But you are moving in a different direction, one that heads toward growth and accomplishment instead of frustration.

There is every reason to believe that, over time, you will just get better and better at using your visual brain, now that you know that you can play to that strength. In a way, there is nothing unique about the last day of the program, because you will be continuing to use what you have learned for the rest of your life.

But completing this whole set of exercises is a big thing. MAKE SURE YOU HAVE YOUR REWARD READY FOR TOMORROW.

Day 28

Activity

Visualize your day, as you do every day. Relax as you do it. Remember: you are good at this!

You have, of course, in your visualization, seen yourself getting your reward. Do you need to make dinner reservations? Do you need to leave work early? Will you be going online today and buying a plane ticket to Bermuda? You must do something today to actualize your reward.

Activity

Relax. Close your eyes.

What are some of your hopes and dreams? Are there things you hoped to accomplish but had given up on because you thought you weren't capable? Are any of those things thinkable now?

Where do you hope to be one month from now? One year from now? Five years from now? Take your time and picture what you want. See yourself—no, *feel* yourself in your new role, or with your new accomplishments. Make those images vivid.

Open your eyes. Are your images clear? If they are not, go back and make sure that they are. Are the images crisp, clear, and specific? Can you retrieve them easily?

Get a small piece of paper, one that you can keep in your wallet and refer to as time passes. Write down your one-month goal, your one-year goal, and your five-year goal.

This is where you are headed.

Congratulations! With your vivid images, and with your ability to hold those images in your mind, you have a powerful tool that is yours forever.

9

On and Off the Wagon?

Don't Waste Another Minute Wondering "Why?"

Arriving in time to refresh her lipstick and review her notes before the start of the 8:30 Monday morning meeting was a new experience for Anna. She felt so professional, so calm and on top of things, and so proud of herself. This was how she always hoped things could be. Without feeling the usual anxiety from arriving just in the nick of time, she didn't have the usual doubt about whether or not she was prepared. She found she was able to think much more clearly and to speak up more often.

On Thursday, she was behind the eight ball again, scrambling at the last minute to have her files in order. She had forgotten that it was her turn to bring snacks to her daughter's preschool class, and by the time she had gotten that arranged, she was running late and cursing at herself. What was the point of trying? What made her think that she'd ever manage to have her act together? Monday had just been a fluke. She might as well give up. She would never be organized.

Anna's "setback" and her reaction to it highlight many common AD/HD experiences. First of all, she took the difficulties on Thursday as evidence that she could not succeed. The fact that she had succeeded on Monday, Tuesday, and Wednesday seemed to have no meaning. Any failure was complete failure. This black-and-white thinking, typical of people with AD/HD, is very demoralizing. What happened to the successes in the first part of the week? They were totally eclipsed by a mistake on Thursday. Anna is only as good as her last failure.

One interesting characteristic of AD/HD thinking, related in part to sensitivity to repeated failures, is a very solid ability to "score" failures, paired with a remarkably poor ability to do the same for successes. This leads to a distorted self-view, and to a large vocabulary of negative self-talk.

Although berated through life with admonitions such as, "If only you'd apply yourself," or "If you just tried a little harder," or "You're just lazy," most people with AD/HD and right-brained thinkers actually try very, very hard. The fact that your efforts don't produce the results that others are looking for is very hurtful and demoralizing. It is often confusing and feels like a personal attack. You work harder than your left-brained peers and most likely feel helpless when told that you simply have to do more. You can't do any more.

Each of these criticisms is like an assault on the self. And since most people are truly doing the best they can most of the time, each of these assaults is experienced almost as a surprise, because it is the context of genuine effort. As if the person with AD/HD were a person with a post-traumatic stress disorder, each personal assault is experienced as a new trauma, triggering the pain of old wounds.

And, as in chronic traumatic stress disorders, the memory of these wounds is not an ordinary memory, laid down as a verbal recollection of past events. Rather, these memories are created and stored in a different way, in fact, in a different part of the brain, and they bring with them all the pain and emotion of the original wound.

So each failure brings with it all the pain of the old failures, overwhelming the emotions and leading to a cascade of self-deprecating self-talk, with its accompanying hopelessness. Each failure is acutely painful and therefore memorable in the nature of traumas. Each pulls off the scab of an old wound, refreshing the pain.

Successes are different. They're not painful, so they're remembered in a normal way. They don't fit very well with the recurrent story of failure. They don't fit into a personal self-history. They are accidents, coincidences, little pieces of good fortune. There is not a coherent story to go with success and no expectation of success. They are more like random events than natural outcomes of legitimate effort. They are easy to forget.

As a result of this pattern, people with AD/HD regularly remember all of their failures and none of their successes. Anna had one bad day after three good days, and it virtually erased, in her mind, and in her emotional view, any progress that she had made. Having tried and failed before, she had gotten used to asking herself a lot of questions to try to understand herself, such as "Why don't I try harder?" "Why don't I ever follow through?" "Why do I make the same mistakes all the time?" and culminating with the usual, "Why do I always sabotage myself?"

We wonder how many millions of hours people with AD/HD have spent in psychotherapy trying to understand why they apparently set themselves up for failure by trying to do things and not following through. They wonder if they are afraid to succeed. They wonder what makes them start out with such good intentions and then not take advantage of the steps that they have taken.

Though we all have personal histories that influence our behavior, for the most part, the kinds of questions Anna is asking of herself, and that so many of you ask of yourselves, will not produce any useful answers. That is because what you are looking at is not neurotic behavior. It is simply neurobiology. That doesn't mean that you shouldn't try to do something about what you observe in yourself. This whole book is about practical suggestions for managing your style of thinking and behavior. It does mean that you should not spend another single minute trying to figure out why you are sabotaging yourself. You are not sabotaging yourself! You are doing the best you can. You just have certain tendencies to have starts and stops, to get off track, and to have difficulties with creating and sticking with sequential activities.

Let us say it again: Trying to figure out what neurotic conflict has you sabotaging yourself is a complete waste of time. There are reasons why you have difficulty with repetition, sequencing, and follow-through. The reasons are neurological, not neurotic. You are doing what anyone with your brain structure would do. So quit punishing yourself. It is worse than a waste of time. It sets you in a negative state of mind, which we know is counterproductive.

There is plenty of information to help you understand why you are the way you are. One way of looking at it is that you are having trouble because, using Thom Hartmann's analogy, you are a better hunter than a farmer. And you are a hunter in a farmer's world, a right-brained adult in a left-brained world. In a different environment, you would have the advantage. (If it makes you feel any better, your strengths are likely to serve you well in our fast-paced, ever-changing, multimedia world.)

Because it's a farmer's world, however, you've been judged according to your weaknesses. It's important not to ignore your weaknesses. In fact, this whole book is about learning to manage the necessary tasks in life by using your strengths to make up for your weaknesses. But it is infinitely more productive to understand, capitalize on, and value your strengths, rather than to evaluate only your weaknesses.

Focus on Your Strengths

Some interesting work by Marcus Buckingham and Donald O. Clifton, PhD, using Gallup Organization analysis, focuses on identifying individual strengths. Their definition of a strength is very useful. In their book, *Now, Discover Your Strengths*, they explain that an area of strength is one in which you can regularly expect near-perfect performance.

What a wonderful idea. They elaborate by explaining that although you can strengthen areas of weakness, you can never bring them up to the performance level in your area of strength. We couldn't agree more. Of course we are helping you manage your areas of weakness. But we want you to stop dwelling on them. They are not who you are.

You are someone who has some exceptional abilities along with some troublesome deficits. That's all the problem is.

Hard Is Easy and Easy Is Hard

One of the interesting things that happens when people do not accurately and consciously identify their strengths is that they take those abilities for granted. This adds to the tendency of AD/HD people to ignore their successes. They also ignore their gifts. Why shouldn't they—they've been working so hard in other areas, their strengths have been devalued and ignored.

Creative, right-brained people with AD/HD have produced some of the most phenomenal breakthroughs in science and culture. They have changed our entire world. People like da Vinci, Edison, Einstein, and Churchill have been innovators, artists, creators, and leaders. They are not typical left-brained thinkers. They have produced work that staggers the mind and elicits admiration. But, did you know, for example, that Churchill was last in his high school class? Or that Einstein was kicked out of school as a young child? A recent Nobel Prize winner in chemistry related that he got a D in high school chemistry.

Many children who think in these ways can be very mathematically minded and able to figure out how to solve problems in geometry and calculus on their own, not following the steps in the textbook. In fact, often they cannot show their steps, leading to failing grades. From a left-brain point of view, those steps are essential. They *are* the work. From a right-brain perspective, getting to the right answer is what counts.

Learning the steps from the textbook and reproducing them is in many ways easier than creating the math from scratch. So, what the right-brained thinker can do easily is difficult for left-brained thinkers. And what left-brained thinkers can do easily is very difficult for right-brained people with AD/HD. Unfortunately, these supposedly easy things are, in many ways, the basics. They are the preliminary steps, and there is a sense that a person must be able to perform the simple tasks first before going on to the more complex ones. This does not always match a person's actual ability, but it is easy to see how it is the accepted wisdom.

You may be able to analyze your company's financial strengths and weaknesses, make proposals for allocation of millions of dollars of assets, and project one-, five-, and ten-year profits, yet not be able to balance your own checkbook. You might be able to write a novel but be unable to plan and prepare a meal.

On another level, a person entering the job market is expected to begin with basic tasks. Those are the most difficult for people with AD/HD and visual thinking. Though their talents might best be used in the higher levels of a company where complex problems are solved and creative solutions are required, they might be stuck in the mail room and file room forever, not being promoted because they can't master those basic tasks. As we said, easy is hard, and hard is easy.

So, when you find yourself having difficulty staying focused on your organizational strategies, remember that these are actually the most difficult things for you. There is no need to punish yourself for having difficulty with something that is difficult.

None of Your Effort Is Wasted

Remember that you have to credit yourself with your efforts, not just your results. Every minute that you spend working on your visualization skills brings you benefits. Every minute that you use to strengthen your visualization skills makes it easier to use them to stay focused, effective, and organized.

If you lose track, that is only part of the process. You are actually farther along than you were before you lost track! You've gained experience. Since you've already done it once, you can feel confident that the next time you try it, you will do at least a little better. You can think about it as a rehearsal, making your next performance likely to be better. Each movement is a step in the right direction.

Fear of Success?

Another reason to focus on the process, not the product, is to give yourself some insurance against pressure to perform. Having positive expectations is a great way to set yourself on a positive track. You want to feel energetic and optimistic. And if you get praise from others around you for your achievements, this can add to your sense of satisfaction and accomplishment.

Sometimes, praise can have a paradoxical effect in people who are very sensitive to those around them. It doesn't feel good to be seen as a failure or to feel the disappointment in those around you. And with expectations for you set quite low, not much is expected of you, either. But with praise comes the sense that you should repeat your performance. All of a sudden, a pressure that was never there before is present. A certain amount of urgency helps galvanize an AD/HD person. But the pressure to perform often promotes fear and self-consciousness, both of which inhibit performance. Success may seem like a hazard.

You may be used to proving that you can be the best at being the worst, since that is all you were able to do. Now, you must re-adjust your self-image. You are not the best, and you are not the worst. You are only human. Sometimes you will succeed, and some-times you will not. Work to absorb the praise you get as fuel to pro-pel you forward. What actually happens, however, is not a measure of who you are. It is only a step along the way.

Is There a Gender Gap?

We have used examples of men and women throughout this book. We have not used men to demonstrate one sort of issue and women to illustrate another, because both men and women with AD/HD and visual thinking are subject to the same difficulties and have had the same sorts of experiences. It used to be thought, in fact, that AD/HD was more common in boys than in girls. We now know that boys tend to be more hyperactive than girls, and girls tend to be more inattentive. We also know that gender roles and ex-pectations provide outlets for girls to perform and to please others that are not traditionally available to boys. This makes it harder to identify girls with AD/HD. But it is thought that there are no signifi-cant differences in the number of males and females with AD/HD.

There are, however, differences in how men and women use mental health help. Traditionally, it has been much more acceptable for a woman to accept help. It is acceptable for women to be weak or helpless or to need assistance. Women learn to be the carriers of emotions in families, and it is acceptable for women to show and express their emotions.

But men are supposed to be the fixers and the helpers. They do not measure up if they show too much emotion. They are supposed to have the answers, and they are not supposed to need help. (This is evidenced by the familiar refusal to ask for directions when lost.) It is a sign of failure to need help, especially emotional help. Men are often pressured into seeking help by the women in their lives. Often, they seek help under threat of loss of the relationship. In other words, it has to get really bad for a lot of men to be able to acknowledge difficulty. It is a clear sign of failure not to know what to do.

Many men think that spending too much time being introspective and thinking about feelings is unproductive. And if they feel emotional, it makes them feel weak. Since visual thinkers are already more sensitive, men who have this sensitivity are at extra risk when acknowledging their failings. As a result, it is natural for them to push away feelings of weakness. Feelings of failure are doubly troublesome. It is not okay to be a failure. And it is not okay to feel bad about it, either!

The risks associated with feeling like a failure make it difficult for many men to even acknowledge deficits. And it can make it difficult for them to try something new. Taking in new information is like a confirmation that they didn't know it in the first place and adds to the feeling of failure. The extra sensitivity of the visual thinker puts men with AD/HD at great risk of never being able to tolerate the pain of recognizing their difficulties. Even if they do identify their difficulties, the expectation of performance is a great roadblock to setting realistic goals and accepting normal progress. This makes change pretty close to impossible.

As a man, you have a choice. You can, bit by bit, tolerate the discomfort of not knowing, the vulnerability of needing to learn, and the real frustration of uneven progress. Or you can continue to believe that you have the answers, despite your difficulties.

What we can say to help you through the discomfort of feeling too many feelings, especially feelings of failure, is that you can learn to be suspicious of your feelings. As an extra sensitive, visual person, you can assume that many of the feelings that you have are more extreme than is really called for by the situation. You can assume that the hurt feelings you get around other people are unrealistic and extreme. You can assume that you see too much, feel too much, interpret too much, and attribute too much to other people. You can assume that your feelings that they judge you harshly are inaccurate. And you can assume that your harsh judgment of yourself is inaccurate, as well. Learning to be suspicious of your sensitivities will allow you to tolerate more of your feelings and will leave you less vulnerable to the frustrations of learning something new and of performing less than perfectly.

For women, there is a different sort of problem as a result of social roles and expectations. Despite changes in women's status and accomplishments, it is still relatively acceptable (relative to men, that is) for women to need help. For disorganized AD/HD women, this means that it is easier for them to slip into a helpless or inadequate role, allowing others to fill in for what they could be expected to do for themselves. Though getting a lot of help brings some real relief, it has a serious risk. By not working out their organizational muscles, women who have accepted their helpless identity relinquish the hope of progress. Along with that, they relinquish control of changing their own lives.

We recognize that homemaking is a difficult role for AD/HD

women. There is no beginning and no end to it, no outside structure, little praise and gratitude, no paycheck or promotion, and no time off! And we know that the standard of treatment for adult AD/HD includes getting outside help for tasks with which a person has serious difficulty. But we are talking about personal responsibility and growth. The risk for women who adopt a more helpless role is that they also become more hopeless, lose self-esteem, and close off opportunities to make progress.

Your Mission, Should You Choose to Accept It

You will not have a straight trajectory. You will have good days and bad days. You will make progress, and then you will lose ground. That is the nature of your nervous system. (It is also the nature of real life itself.)

But if you practice building skill in your area of strength, and if you learn to understand why you are the way you are, you will find your own ways of staying clear, focused, and organized. All you have to do is try. Because you've got the basic ability, and we think you're up to it.

Using your strengths instead of weaknesses gives you a unique opportunity to take control of areas of your life that have been creating chaos and disorganization. These simple, practical, and effective techniques can be applied to any area of your life, and they get easier to use and more powerful the more you use them. You can't lose them, misplace them, or forget them. You don't have to renew them or reorder them. They are yours, forever.

Appendix

Medications for Treatment of AD/HD

Manipulation of neurotransmitter levels is the mechanism of virtually all psychiatric medications. These medications vary in the way they accomplish this, the length of time that they work, their speed of efficacy, and their specificity. They have, along with these differences, different kinds of side effects, drug interactions, precautions, and adverse effects.

The unpredictable levels of focus and attention of Attention Deficit Disorder with or without Hyperactivity are due to unpredictable levels of specific neurotransmitters. By improving the levels of neurotransmitters, we can usually regulate the levels of focus and attention. In general, our goal is to boost the levels of those neurotransmitters, with norepinephrine and dopamine as our main targets.

This summary of medication treatments cannot replace an evaluation by a qualified medical professional. It is intended to help you be an informed consumer and patient.

Categories of Medications

As of this writing, the two main categories of medications for treatment of AD/HD are stimulants and nonstimulants. As we advance our understanding of AD/HD, more categories may be added. But this basic division exists because of the history of both the diagnosis and of the treatment of AD/HD.

AD/HD was first called "hyperkinesis," referring to children who showed too much activity. Overly active, distractible children calmed down when given stimulant medications, and then they were able to focus and concentrate. The diagnosis of the condition was made based on the child's response to treatment with stimulants.

It makes sense that treatment with psychostimulants, or stimulants as we now call them, became the main treatment for hyperkinesis. After all, this class of medication was an integral part of the diagnosis. The medications are called stimulants because they do cause alertness and arousal. However, the efficacy of these medications is separate from the stimulant effect that they have on many people. The medications work by stimulating production and release of the neurotransmitters necessary for focus and control. The alertness and jitteriness that some people experience when taking stimulants is actually a side effect of AD/HD treatment. And, because these medications stimulate the neurotransmitters that promote control, most people with AD/HD calm down when they take them.

There are other medications that also increase levels of needed neurotransmitters but don't have the stimulant effects, and so this broad category is referred to as nonstimulants. All that this means, really, is that we have the category of stimulants, and the category of "everything else." The everything-else category has a specific treatment for AD/HD, antidepressants, as well as a variety of other medications.

One Size Doesn't Fit All

The early history of treatment of AD/HD, along with the stereotype of the hyperactive boy throwing spitballs, creates the impression that AD/HD treatment equals Ritalin®. But, just as there are many different symptom pictures for people with AD/HD, there are many treatment regimens. If you pursue medication to treat your AD/HD, you may need to try several different treatments before you find what works for you. You may find that a single treatment works for you, or you may do better with a combination of treatments.

Some people do very well on stimulants, such as methylphenidate or amphetamines. Others have side effects from these medications that are too uncomfortable to live with; these may include appetite suppression, irritability, and muscle tension.

Because stimulants are drugs that are abused, these are highly regulated by the U.S. Drug Enforcement Administration. Some people find it too cumbersome to manage getting prescriptions for a controlled substance.

From a purely pharmacologic point of view, stimulants are highly effective at treating the core symptoms of AD/HD, including distractibility, impulsivity, difficulty initiating difficult tasks, and problems with follow-through. On the other hand, the stimulant effects of these medications affect some people too greatly for them to be able to take a dose that will effectively treat their AD/HD symptoms. Also, some have strong reactions when the medication wears off. This often causes a rebound phenomenon, resulting in irritability and even stronger AD/HD symptoms.

A significant advantage that nonstimulant medications have

over stimulants is that many of them last a lot longer. Plus, they aren't controlled substances, and have the advantage of being easier to obtain. Many provide important relief from some of the more internal symptoms of AD/HD, such as worry and irritability. And they can help slow down thinking in way that benefits the visual, right-brained thinker.

Though it is possible, to some degree, to predict the probability that any one treatment will be effective, the reality is that there is no way to know for sure how any one medication will affect you until you try it.

The following is a description of the different medications we use to treat AD/HD. It is not meant as a prescribing guide, but rather as an orientation.

Stimulants

There are quite a few different stimulants, most of which come in different dosage forms. Compared to many other medications that have a fairly standard dose for most adults, dosing of stimulants is highly variable and your doctor should individualize it. A medication with a dosage range from one milligram to sixty milligrams must be administered with attention and care.

Methylphenidate comes in a number of forms—some generic, some brand name. It acts in about twenty minutes and generally lasts three to four hours. Ironically, we give this short-acting medication to people who can't remember things! Therefore, the long-acting forms of this medication have been a huge benefit to most patients.

These medications have various names:

- Ritalin® is the well-known brand name of methylphenidate.
- Ritalin LA® is a time-release capsule. Half of the medication is released immediately, and the other half takes longer to dissolve (about four hours later).
- Concerta® is methylphenidate in the Oros® delivery system. This system uses an insoluble capsule with an interior that absorbs moisture. As it does, the medication is slowly released. It lasts longer than the time-release capsules, generally about twelve hours. The initial dose that is released is lower than in the time-release capsules, and the dose at the end of the twelve hours tends to be a little bit higher.
- Metadate® is another time-release preparation that's designed to deliver one-third of the dose initially and two-thirds over the course of the next several hours. It lasts about eight hours.
- Focalin® is an interesting medication. It is the d-isomer of methylphenidate. Most molecules have a left and a right form, or an l and a d form. These are mirror images of each other. It turns out that for many therapeutic molecules, only one of these isomers is the active component. Medications containing only the active isomer tend to be a little more potent and have slightly fewer side effects than the mixture.
- Focalin LA® uses the same time-release method as Ritalin LA®.
- Daytrana® is methylphenidate in a daily patch. The medica-

tion is released very smoothly, though a bit slowly at the outset, and there seem to be fewer side effects than with oral medications, other than the possibility of a skin rash from the patch.

Amphetamines are the other general class of stimulants:

- Dextroamphetamine, known by the trade name Dexedrine®, is the D-isomer of amphetamine. In its generic form, it is available as a tablet and lasts about four hours. The brand-name product comes in a time-release capsule, which lasts about six to eight hours.
- Adderall® is a mixture of four amphetamine salts. In its immediate-release form, it lasts about four hours. It is available as a generic. For most people, this mixture provides more efficacy than dextroamphetamine alone. For many, however, it has more side effects.
- Adderall XR® is a time-release formulation, with half of the medication released immediately, and the other half released about four hours later.
- Desoxyn® is methamphetamine. When made in illegal labs, it has led to terrible drug abuse, but the pharmacological preparation is pure and effective nonetheless. Interestingly, it has fewer side effects than the other amphetamines for many people. At the present time, there is no generic formulation and no time-release formulation. Desoxyn® lasts about three to four hours.

Nonstimulants

Strattera® is a medication specifically indicated for the treatment of AD/HD, and at the present time is the only nonstimulant specifically approved for treatment of AD/HD. Similar to an antidepressant in the way it works, it blocks removal of the needed neurotransmitters. Like most of the nonstimulant treatments, this medication takes a bit of time to reach its maximum efficacy. For most people, the benefits last around the clock, so there is little rebound or sudden return of AD/HD symptoms.

Though very helpful for many people with the emotional components of AD/HD, such as constant worrying and irritability, it may not be as potent as the stimulants in helping people get started with difficult tasks. But, because AD/HD is in itself full of unpredictability and chaos, a medication that works evenly and consistently can be extremely beneficial.

Buproprion, also sold as Wellbutrin®, is an antidepressant targeting both dopamine and norepinephrine levels. A very effective antidepressant, for many people this medication provides noticeable reduction in AD/HD symptoms. Although for most people not as powerful as other treatments in treating all the symptoms of AD/HD, for some it represents the best combination of efficacy with low side effects. As of this writing, buproprion is being evaluated for a specific indication for AD/HD.

Modafinil, sold as Provigil®, is used for relief of daytime sleepiness from narcolepsy or the sleep deprivation of shift work. Its exact mechanism of action is unknown, and it doesn't produce typical stimulant effects. It does, however, increase overall alertness, and for some people, this increase in arousal will relieve many symptoms of AD/HD. For others, it is not as effective. This medication is now the subject of research to clarify its efficacy in treating AD/HD.

Guanfacine, sold as Tenex®, and clonidine, sold as Catapres®, are medications that are approved for lowering blood pressure. Because they regulate norepinephrine, these medications are sometimes used to calm hyperactivity and to promote sleep for those who have insomnia from taking stimulant medications. These are not first-line drugs for treating AD/HD.

Tricyclic antidepressants, such as imipramine, desipramine, and nortriptyline, work on many neurotransmitters, including dopamine and norepinephrine. Because they work on so many other neurological pathways, they have many side effects. However, when taken at much lower doses than those needed to treat depression, they can be very helpful for symptoms of AD/HD.

Emsam® is a new form of an old antidepressant, selegiline. It is an MAO inhibitor (monoamine oxidase inhibitor) meaning it inhibits reuptake of a number of neurotransmitters. MAO inhibitors are very effective antidepressants, with a very serious side effect that has sent them to the back of the physician's shelf. When a person who takes them eats the wrong foods, they can have a potentially fatal elevation in blood pressure. However, Emsam® is selegiline in patch form, and at the lowest dose, there are no dietary restrictions. Old research on selegiline showed efficacy in treating AD/HD. This makes sense, as selegiline increases dopamine along with norepinephrine and serotonin. This medication is only FDA-indicated for depression. But, used with discretion when other medications are not effective, in some cases it can be a useful tool for treatment of AD/HD.

Some physicians are using amantadine, an interesting medication that increases dopamine. Edward Hallowell and John Ratey's *Delivered from Distraction* has an interesting section on the experimental use of amantadine. Again, it is not FDA approved for treatment of AD/HD, but seems to be a good choice for some people who cannot tolerate stimulants but need a dopamine boost to get them motivated.

Bibliography

Amen, Daniel. *Change Your Brain, Change Your Life*. New York: Times Books, 2000.

———. *Healing ADD: The Breakthrough Program That Allows You to See and Heal the 6 Types of ADD*. New York: Putnam and Sons, 2001.

Barkley, Russell A. *Attention-Deficit Hyperactivity Disorder: A Handbook for Diagnosis and Treatment*. 2nd ed. New York: Guilford Press, 1998.

Baynes, Kathleen. "Human Neurobiology: Split-Brain Research." *Science* 280, no. 5365 (May 1998): 902–5.

Bower, Bruce. "Whole-Brain Interpreter: Michael Gazzaniga." *Science News* 149 (February 1996): 124–25.

Brown, Thomas. *Attention-Deficit Disorder and Comorbidities in Children, Adolescents, and Adults*. Washington, DC: American Psychiatric Press, 2000.

Buckingham, Marcus, and Donald Clifton. *Now, Discover Your Strengths*. New York: Free Press, 2001.

Buckner, Randy L., et al. "Study Captures Images of Memories Being Formed in the Human Brain." *Science* 281, no. 5380 (August 1998).

Coull, Jennifer T., and Anna C. Nobre. "Where and When to Pay Attention: The Neural Systems for Directing Attention to Spatial Locations and to Time Intervals as Revealed by Both PET and fMRI." *Journal of Neuroscience* 18 (September 1998): 7426–35.

Davis, Ronald. *The Gift of Dyslexia*. Burlingame, CA: Ability Workshop Press, 1994.

Edwards, Betty. *Drawing on the Right Side of the Brain*. Los Angeles: Jeremy P. Tarcher, 1989.

Ernst, Monique, Alan J. Zametkin, John A. Matochik, Peter H. Jons, and Robert M. Cohen. "DOPA Decoarboxylase Activity in Attention Deficit Disorder Adults: A [Fluorine-18] Fluorodopa Positron Emission Tomographic Study." *Journal of Neuroscience* 18, no. 15 (August 1998): 5901–7.

Ferres, Leo. "Speech Perception and Lateralization." Final Paper: Basics of Neuroscience, Carleton University.

Funnell, M. G., P. M. Corballis, and M. S. Gazzaniga. "Hemispheric Processing Asymmetries: Implications for Memory." *Brain Cognition* 46, nos.1–2 (June 2001): 135–39.

Gardner, Howard. *Frames of Mind: The Theory of Multiple Intelligences*. New York: Basic Books, 1983.

Gladwell, Malcolm. "Java Man: How Caffeine Created the Modern World." *New Yorker*, July 30, 2001.

Gmeindl, Leon. "Lateralization of Executive Processes in the Human Brain." University of Michigan. (website)

Grandin, Temple. "My Experiences with Visual Thinking, Sensory Problems, and Communication Difficulties." Center for the Study of Autism, June 2000. http://www.autism.org/temple/visual.html.

Hallowell, Edward M., and John J. Ratey. *Delivered from Distraction: Getting the Most Out of Life with Attention Deficit Disorder*. New York: Ballantine, 2005.

———. *Driven to Distraction: Recognizing and Coping with Attention Deficit Disorder from Childhood through Adulthood*. New York: Pantheon, 1994.

Hartmann, Thom. *ADD: A Different Perception*. Grass Valley, CA: Underwood Books, 1997.

Kelly, Kate, and Peggy Ramundo. *You Mean I'm Not Lazy, Stupid, or Crazy? A Self-Help Book for Adults with Attention Deficit Disorder*. New York: Fireside, 1993.

Kohlberg, Judith, and Kathleen Nadeau. *ADD-Friendly Ways to Organize Your Life*. New York: Brunner-Routledge, 2002.

Mate, Gabor. *Scattered: How Attention Deficit Disorder Originates and What You Can Do about It*. New York: Dutton, 1999.

Miller, Earl K., and Jonathan D. Cohen. "An Integrative Theory of Prefrontal Cortex Function." *Annual Review of Neuroscience* 24 (2002): 167–202.

Mizoguchi, Kazushige, Mitsutoshi Yuzurihara, Atsushi Ishige, Hiroshi Sasaki, De-Hua Chui, and Takeshi Tabira. "Chronic Stress Induces Impairment of Spatial Working Memory because of Prefrontal Dopaminergic Dysfunction." *Journal of Neuroscience* 20, no. 4 (February 2001): 1568–74.

Pinker, Steven. *How the Mind Works*. New York: Norton, 1997.

———. *The Language Instinct: How the Mind Creates Language*. New York: William Morrow, 1994.

Ratey, John J. *A User's Guide to the Brain*. New York: Pantheon, 2001.

Schweitzer, Julie B., Tracy L. Faber, Scott T. Grafton, Larry E. Tune, John M. Hoffman, and Clinton D. Kilts. "Alterations in the Functional Anatomy of Working Memory in Adult Attention Deficit Hyperactivity Disorder." *American Journal of Psychiatry* 157 (February 2000): 278–80.

Shlain, Leonard. *The Alphabet versus the Goddess: The Conflict between Word and Image*. New York: Viking, 1998.

Silverman, Linda Kreger. *Upside-Down Brilliance: The Visual-Spatial Learner*. Glendale, CO: DeLeon, 2002.

Specter, Michael. "Rethinking the Brain: How the Songs of Canaries Upset a Fundamental Principle of Science." *New Yorker*, July 23, 2001.

Wallis, Jonathan D., Kathleen C. Anderson, and Earl K. Miller. "Single Neurons in Prefrontal Cortex Encode Abstract Rules." *Nature* 411, no. 6840 (June 2001): 953–56.

Wender, Paul H. *ADHD: Attention Deficit Hyperactivity Disorder in Children and Adults.* New York: Oxford University Press, 2000.

West, Thomas G. *In the Mind's Eye: Visual Thinkers, Gifted People with Dyslexia and Other Learning Difficulties, Computer Images, and the Ironies of Creativity.* Amherst, NY: Prometheus Books, 1997.

Comprehensive Contents